Yoga: Science of the Absolute

Yoga: Science of the Absolute

A Commentary on the Yoga Sutras of Patanjali

Abbot George Burke
(Swami Nirmalananda Giri)

Light of the Spirit Press
Cedar Crest, New Mexico

Published by
Light of the Spirit Press
lightofthespiritpress.com

Light of the Spirit Monastery
P. O. Box 1370
Cedar Crest, New Mexico 87008
www.OCOY.org

ISBN-13: 978-1-7325266-5-5
ISBN-10: 1-7325266-5-6

Library of Congress Control Number: 2019930951

Bisac Categories:
REL032030 RELIGION / Hinduism / Sacred Writings
PHI033000 PHILOSOPHY / Hindu

021919

Contents

Introduction vii
Samadhi Pada: Yoga Sutras Book I 1
Sadhana Pada: Yoga Sutras Book II 43
Vibhuti Pada: Yoga Sutras Book III 97
Kaivalya Pada: Yoga Sutras Book IV 132
Get Your Free Meditation Guide 165
Glossary 166
About the Author 193
Light of the Spirit Monastery 194
Reading for Awakening 195

INTRODUCTION

The *Yoga Sutras* of Patanjali is the most authoritative text on Yoga as a practice. It is also known as the *Yoga Darshana* because it is the fundamental text of Yoga as a philosophy (though practice is discussed) as one of the six orthodox systems (darshanas) of Sanatana Dharma, the Eternal Religion.

The basis of Sanatana Dharma

There is a temptation to designate a single book as the greatest or most important book in the the world. The Yoga Darshana is one of these, but in reality it is one of thirteen texts upon which the totality of authentic Sanatana Dharma is based. When those texts are studied and applied, then a person is a Sanatana Dharmi: not a "member" or "adherent" of Sanatana Dharma, but an embodiment of dharma, one who is moving toward the ultimate goal of liberation. The thirteen texts are:

1. Isha Upanishad
2. Kena Upanishad
3. Katha Upanishad
4. Prashna Upanishad
5. Mundaka Upanishad
6. Mandukya Upanishad
7. Taittiriya Upanishad
8. Aitareya Upanishad
9. Chandogya Upanishad
10. Brihadaranyaka Upanishad

11. Shvetashvatara Upanishad
12. Srimad Bhagavad Gita (usually just called "the Gita")
13. Yoga Darshana (Yoga Sutras)

Since the Yoga Darshana is based on the Sankhya philosophy (darshana), the Sankhya Karika which is its fundamental text could be considered a fourteenth basic text of Sanatana Dharma.

The upanishads are books of varying length setting forth the spiritual realizations of the ancient sages of India based on their experiential knowledge of the Absolute Reality. They are the oldest of the texts listed here. The Bhagavad Gita is a digest of the upanishads, containing philosophical and practical instruction on the way to attain the same experience as the upanishadic sages. The Sankhya Karika is the basic text of the Sankhya Darshan, the philosophy on which both the Gita and the Yoga Darshan are based. The common feature of all these texts is that they are based on verifiable reality, not intellectual theory ("reason") or unverifiable "revelation" by a single historical personage whose existence is not even assured nor is there any way to ensure that the revelation has not been corrupted over the centuries by omissions and interpolations).

There is no need to have "faith" in these texts, for their statements can be verified by any reader, as has been done over thousands of years by countless yogis in India. A virtual army of self-realized men and women have proved their veracity and accuracy. Many of them are living right now as witnesses to the truth of Sanatana Dharma, which is based on the principle that all sentient beings are destined to attain liberation–union with divinity–since they are eternal parts of the Supreme Spirit, the Purushottama.

Sankhya

The Sankhya philosophy is the original philosophy of India, the other darshanas being formulated much, much later. Therefore the thirteen texts listed above are based on the Sankhya philosophy. As already stated, the Sankhya Karika is the most authoritative Sankhya text, being considered a digest of the teachings of the divine sage Kapila Muni ("Among the siddhas [perfected beings] I am the sage Kapila" Bhagavad Gita 10:26.) *A Brief Sanskrit Glossary* defines Sankhya as: "One of the six orthodox systems of Hindu philosophy whose originator was the sage Kapila. Sankhya is the original Vedic philosophy, endorsed by Krishna in the Bhagavad Gita (Gita 2:39; 3:3,5; 18:13,19), the second chapter of which is entitled 'Sankhya Yoga.' The *Ramakrishna-Vedanta Wordbook* says: 'Sankhya postulates two ultimate realities, Purusha and Prakriti. Declaring that the cause of suffering is man's identification of Purusha with Prakriti and its products, Sankhya teaches that liberation and true knowledge are attained in the supreme consciousness, where such identification ceases and Purusha is realized as existing independently in its transcendental nature.' Not surprisingly, then, Yoga is based on the Sankhya philosophy." The Sankhya philosophy is the basis of the Yoga philosophy, for Yoga is a philosophy as well as a practice and the goal.

Patanjali

There are various theories about just who Patanjali was, none of which are provable beyond a doubt. Actually this is no problem, since what matters is the fact that the Yoga Sutras are demonstrably true. As Paramhansa Yogananda said in his autobiography: "Patanjali's date is unknown, though a number of scholars place him in the second century B.C. The rishis gave forth treatises on all subjects with such insight that ages have been powerless to outmode them; yet, to the subsequent consternation of historians, the sages made no effort to attach their own dates and personalities to their literary works. They knew their lives were only temporarily important as flashes of the great infinite Life; and that truth is timeless, impossible to trademark, and no private possession of their own."

We do know that the Nath Yogis, followers of Gorakhnath, claim that Patanjali was one of their Order, as was Jesus.

This commentary

This commentary is not meant to be a scholarly commentary, but a practical one. The translation I have used is that found in *The Science of Yoga* by I. K. Taimni, though I have consulted other translations throughout.

SAMADHI PADA: YOGA SUTRAS BOOK I

1. Now, an exposition of Yoga [is to be made].

This is the usual formula for the beginning of a major text. It is common in most Sanskrit commentaries to interpret *atha* as meaning that there are prerequisites to the studying of sacred subjects, that basic philosophical principles must be first learned, and spiritual disciplines followed, especially moral and ascetic observances. Only then is the student qualified to be taught the wisdom embodied in the text. Commentators say that *atha* is meant to remind them of this fact and to warn them that if they have not laid such a foundation then their study may be defective and fruitless. Agreeing with this, Jnaneshwara Bharati renders this sutra in an explanatory paraphrase: "Now, after having done prior preparation through life and other practices, the study and practice of Yoga begins." We will not now outline what the preparation is, since Patanjali will do so in Book II, the Sadhana Pada, in sutra twenty-nine regarding yama and niyama. The reason he waits is given by Shankara in his commentary: "No one will follow through the practices and restrictions of yoga unless the goal and the related means to it have been clearly set out… as yoga is the result of applying the means to yoga.… Yoga is the goal of the yoga methods."

First, then, we should consider the nature of the state of yoga to which we should be aspiring. Yogananda often said: "Yoga is the beginning of the end," as the capstone of many lives lived in a positive manner, which included a conscious search for God. In this life there must be a continuation of that mode of life to prepare ourselves for the supreme science, the science of the Absolute which we call Yoga.

Yoga requires preparation. This is proven by the fact that after over one hundred years of yoga teaching and practice in the west there has been little lasting effect, for few indeed have ascended to higher consciousness. The reason is the lack of foundation upon which to build an effective spiritual life. One time in a conversation with Sri Anandamayi Ma I told her: "There is no genuine teacher of yoga in America." She nodded her head and replied: "I know it." The yoga peddlers come to town, sell their wares, and move on leaving behind ignorant and confused people trying to get benefit from something completely beyond their capacity. These unfortunates are not negative or unintelligent people, but they are incompetent because they have no background, no preparation, especially in the matter of purification. Patanjali is aware of this, and so his first word in *Yoga Darshan* is *Atha*, to indicate that some purification and discipline is necessary before yoga can be undertaken. This does not mean that the aspirant has to wait until he is proficient in all the observances and avoidances (yama and niyama), but he definitely must understand them, and commit himself to their observance right at the start. Then he will be ready to begin.

In his commentary on this sutra Vyasa states: "Yoga is samadhi," the superconscious state. Commenting on that, Shankara says something different from the usual: "Yoga is not to be taken as from the root *yuj* in the sense of joining together, but the sense of *sam-a-dha*: set together. Yoga is samadhana [samadhi], complete concentration." He makes this assertion because only separate things can be joined. Later he says: "Yoga is the eternal relation with the Self." *Samadhi*-yoga is not the bringing about of the union of the two, but the realization of their eternal unity. This is no small point. "The Self is always in samadhi," says Shankara.

Because of their supreme authority, Vyasa and Shankara will be quoted a great deal in this commentary. Although much that they say is quite technical, it is impossible to responsibly and completely bring out the meaning of the Yoga Sutras otherwise.

2. Yoga is the inhibition of the modifications of the mind. *Yogash chitta-vritti-nirodhah.*

Chitta is the subtle energy that is the substance of the mind, and therefore the mind itself. Vritti is a thought-wave, mental modification, mental whirlpool, a ripple in the chitta. Nirodha is restraint, restriction, suppression, or dissolving.

Some say that chitta-vritti-nirodha means cessation of the modifications of the mind, some that it means control of the vrittis or thoughts, some that it is the suppression, destruction or erasing of vrittis, some that it is the lessening or inhibition or restricting of vrittis, and some that it is the silencing of the mind.

Certainly nirodha embraces all of these, but only as aspects or stages toward the ultimate nirodha. These stages deal with the vrittis themselves, and sometimes with an interaction with them to affect them in some way. In all of these the vrittis have already arisen, so they are simply ways of dealing with them. These stages are only police-actions, cleanup operations, and are not at all the answer. The answer is for the chitta to be in such a state that vrittis *cannot* arise. Then alone will there be no problems to deal with. There is no lasting value in producing a state where the arising of the vrittis is only prevented, because if there is a lapse they will start up all over again and we will be right back where we started. I have seen this a lot over the years, and in time it leads to frustration and surrender to the condition.

The nirodha Patanjali is presenting to us is a permanent condition of the chitta in which it has been so transformed or transmuted that the arising of vrittis is *impossible*; it just cannot happen. Sri Ramana Maharshi spoke of this as a state in which the mind has become the Self. Until then, he said, all other attempts are like catching a thief, making him a policeman, and ordering him to go catch himself. It cannot work. It is the difference between birth-control and sterility. Nirodha is the latter.

When we realize this, our whole perspective on yoga will change, and so will our evaluation of our practice. First of all, vrittis are not just thoughts, they are also impressions and impulses. Thoughts are actually the least of the modifications of the chitta. But most important, vrittis are *responses* of the chitta, called forth by external or internal stimuli. These are the major problems, though the real, fundamental problem is the capacity of the mind to respond in modifications of any kind. We can see from this that to think nirodha is just a matter of no-thought is missing the point entirely. Yoga is the radical transformation of the very nature of the mind, and therefore of its functions. It is not just taming or training it. That leads nowhere in the long run.

Having said this, I must point out, as does Shankara, that there is a state known as nirodha samadhi in which the mind enters into the perfectly non-responsive condition. In the beginning this is a temporary state, but when practiced enough it becomes permanent, unbroken. Shankara declares that "moksha [liberation] is not something different from nirodha samadhi. There is some distinction insofar as after nirodha samadhi there is recurrence of active mental processes [pravritti], whereas moksha is a final cessation [nivritti] of them. But in that samadhi as such, there is no distinction from moksha. So the sutra [1:3] has said, 'Then the seer is established in his own nature,' and it will also be said [4:34] that being established in its own nature is moksha: 'or it is the establishment of the power-of-consciousness in its own nature.' So it is incontestable that the sutra means to say that moksha is only by seedless [nirbija] samadhi."

3. Then the seer [drashta] is established in his own essential and fundamental nature [swarupa].

Vyasa immediately comments and paraphrases: "Then the power-of-consciousness [chit-shakti] rests in its own nature, as in the state of release [moksha]. But when the mind is extraverted [turned outward], though it is so, it is not so." That is, even though each of us always rests in his true nature, for it is inviolable, at the same time we do not so rest experientially. Quite the opposite; we are aware of and identify with just about everything else.

Shankara first says in consideration of this sutra: "It has been said that yoga is inhibition of the mental processes, by which inhibition the true being of the purusha as the cognizer is realized." Though a bit convoluted, the following words of Shankara are very important: "Purusha is the cognizer of buddhi in the sense that he is aware of buddhi in its transformations as the forms of the mental processes. The nature of the purusha is simple awareness of them; the one who is aware is not different from the awareness. If the one who is aware were different from the awareness itself, he would be changeable and then would not be a mere witness who has objects shown to him."

Self-forgetfulness is the root of all our problems, the essence of samsara itself. Consciousness (chaitanya) is our essential nature. When asked what the Self is, Sri Ramakrishna simply answered: "The witness of the mind." We are the seer of our individual life in the same way that God is the Seer of cosmic life. Therefore Patanjali speaks of the Self as the Seer. When the chitta remains in a state both free from modifications and from the state in which is is possible for modifications to occur, then the yogi is established in his swarupa, essential form or nature. In that state his swarupa is that which imparts to him perfect knowledge of himself. So it is not just Seeing, it is Knowing.

People are getting flashes or glimpses of their Self throughout their lives, but they are overshadowed and even eclipsed by their usual perceptions of the modifications of the chitta. That is why it is necessary for us to reach that state (sthiti) in which no modifications can take place, but we remain firmly in the consciousness of our reality, just as does God.

4. In other states there is assimilation/identification [of the seer] with the modifications [of the mind].

Outside the state of being centered fully in the Self, there is *vritti sarupyam*–such a close identity with the experiences of relative existence that the person seems to be assimilated by them, overshadowed and rendered completely forgetful by them, mistaking them for reality and for his Self-nature. This is the state of being "lost" from which we must become "saved." But unlike popular religion (and all religions provide "saviors" of some sort), Yoga explains to us that we must save ourselves–through Yoga. "Therefore, be a yogi" (Bhagavad Gita 6:46).

Fortunately, we do not really change when this false identity occurs. As Shankara points out: "The apparent change is not intrinsic but projected [adhyaropita], like a crystal's taking on the color of something put near it."

Here is another paragraph from Shankara that I think is important both for its accuracy and for the fact of it being said by such an authority: "Therefore knowledge of objective forms, and memory, and its recall, and effort and desire and so on, are all essentially not-self [anatma], because they are objects of knowledge like outer forms, and because they exist-for-another [parartha] as is shown by their dependence on the body-mind aggregate for the manifestation of their forms and other qualities. So because they have dependence, and are impermanent and are accompanied by effort–for these and similar reasons it is certain that they are essentially not-self." This is also important because it is identical with the teaching of Buddha on these points, showing that Buddha was a classical Sankhya Yogi and not a "Buddhist" at all.

There is a most important point that must be pointed out here. Patanjali tells us that we must bring the chitta, the mind-substance, into a state of pure clarity in which modifications can no longer be produced. Why does he not tell us to just jettison the mind and be rid of it? Because, as both Vyasa and Shankara state in their commentaries on this sutra, the purusha has an eternal, "beginningless relation" with the mind. We have always had it and always will, so we must correct/perfect it through yoga to be freed from samsara.

5. The modifications [vritti] of the mind are five-fold and are painful [klishta] or not painful [aklishta].

The five types of modification will be listed in the next sutra, but right now Patanjali wants us to know that they all can be painful or not painful.

However, there is a whole other way of looking at these modifications, and that is held by both Vyasa and Shankara. It interprets klishta and aklishta as "tainted by the kleshas" and "untainted by the kleshas." The kleshas are ignorance, egotism, attractions and repulsions towards objects, and desperate clinging to physical life from the fear of death. They will be considered in detail in sutras two through nine of the second section of the Yoga Sutras. So the modifications of the chitta can be either tainted (impure) or untainted (pure). Obviously this is going to determine their effect on us.

Vyasa says this: "The tainted [modifications] are caused by the five kleshas; they become the seed-bed for the growth of the accumulated karma seed-stock. The others are pure and are the field of Knowledge. They oppose involvement in the gunas. They remain pure even if they occur in a stream of tainted ones. In gaps between tainted ones, there are pure ones; in gaps between pure ones, tainted ones. It is only by mental processes that samskaras corresponding to them are produced, and by samskaras are produced new mental processes. Thus the wheel of mental process and samskara revolves. Such is the mind. But when it gives up its involvement, it abides in the likeness of the Self." Commenting on Vyasa's comment, Shankara says: "Ignorance and the other taints become the seed-bed for tainted mental processes. When these last appear, the karma seed-stock is near to ripening."

Shankara relates this situation to yoga practice, saying: "Only by recourse to practice and detachment, which oppose them *en bloc*, does inhibition [nirodhah] succeed; their mere number does not make inhibition impossible, though there is no effective means of inhibiting them one by one." This is very important, because one of the tricks of the mind is to tell us that we need to "work up" to the right state or tackle our defects only one-by-one. But those who accept this wrong way of going about clearing their lives and consciousness end up failing completely, as was the ego's intention when it suggested it so "reasonably." Rather, Shankara tells us that yoga practice assaults the whole bundle of mental illusions at once, just as one army attacks another army *en masse*, not just soldier by soldier. This is heartening news, for it assures us that yoga acts as a general antidote to the poison of the kleshas, like a wide-spectrum antibiotic attacks all forms of infection at once.

6. [The five kinds of modifications are] right knowledge [pramana], wrong knowledge [viparyaya], fancy [vikalpa], sleep [nidra], and memory [smritaya].

Each of these merits an individual consideration.

Pramana includes the means of valid knowledge, logical proof, and the means of right perception. Although logical proof is listed here, it is usually held that pramana also includes experiential proof such as proven intuition or yogic perception that has been investigated and shown to be accurate. Although Taimni and most translators render this "right knowledge," it is actually *the means* to right knowledge.

Viparyaya is erroneous perception, wrong knowledge, illusion, misapprehension, and distraction of mind: the means to wrong knowledge. In Sankhya philosophy, the basis of Yoga, it is said that viparyaya is caused by ignorance (avidya), egoism (asmita), attachment (raga), antipathy (dwesha), and self-love in the sense of clinging to life (abhinivesha).

Vikalpa is imagination, fantasy, mental construct, abstraction, conceptualization, hallucination, distinction, experience, thought and oscillation of the mind.

Nidra is sleep, either dreaming or dreamless, but in the Yoga Sutras it means dreamless sleep alone.

Smritaya is memory and recollection.

All mental phenomena fall into one of these classifications. It is interesting to see that just as there are five senses, so there are five modifications of the mind.

Now Patanjali looks at each in turn.

7. [Facts of] right knowledge [are based on] direct cognition, inference, or testimony.

Pramana has three bases: direct perception, inference, and what Jnaneshwara Bharati calls "testimony or verbal communication from others who have knowledge." All commentators say that this latter includes scriptural texts. Nevertheless, the first listed by Patanjali is pratyaksha–personal perception. This is quite logical in a text on yoga, for the purpose of yoga is the gaining of direct knowledge. Next he lists logical inference (anumana), either our own or another's. Last comes scriptural testimony. So we see a hierarchy of values. Most valued is our personal insight, next is our logical thought or that of someone we are communicating with, and last is the written text. This is because a living process is always more valuable, and also because the written text may be defective in some way. So scriptures come last, a feature unique to Sanatana Dharma.

8. Wrong knowledge is a false conception of a thing whose real form does not correspond to such a mistaken conception.

We all have experience of mistaken perception. Sometimes in a boat it looks and feels as if the shore is moving and the boat is standing still. Those of us who have ridden a train very much will recall feeling that the train we were sitting in was moving, only to find out that it was the train next to us that moved. We often "see" wrongly. For example, I had a cousin that did not look like me at all. Yet, my friends would see him on the street and call out or start speaking to him, thinking he was me. And the same would happen to me with his friends.

When as a child I went to the movies I would experience three things that really disturbed me at the time. First, when the sound came on I could clearly perceive that it came from speakers on two sides of the theater, yet after a short while the sound would not only seem to be coming from the screen, it would seem to come from the mouths of the actors! Second, in motion pictures where carriage or wagon wheels were shown, at certain speeds the spokes would appear to reverse their direction and be moving backwards. Third, if I had seen a movie or a feature before, when I saw it again it seemed to last only about half the time it had the first time. So I realized that sound, sight, and time sense could be altered and were not absolutely true. After a while I came to understand that most of my experience was viparyaya in some form.

The only remedy for viparyaya is to experience things as they really are. And that is one of the purposes of yoga. In fact, Shankara said that "inhibition of illusion must precede that of the others, since it is their root."

9. An image conjured up by words without any substance behind it is fancy [vikalpa].

Here "words" can mean internal thought as well external speaking, either by ourselves or by others. We all experience having a mixture of both right and wrong ideas about something. That is viparyaya as in the previous sutra. But vikalpa is completely without basis or substance. Shankara is fond of using the simile of the horns of a rabbit, since such things just do not exist. Interestingly, some time before I became a yogi I read a psychological study by a man who knew of a culture somewhere in the western hemisphere where the people all believe that rabbits have horns. He even went "rabbit watching" with them and was amazed that they all swore fervently to him that the rabbits he was seeing without horns really did have horns: they could see them.

Here we see the danger of lying. In time our minds will habitually function in vikalpa and we will begin lying to ourselves. A hallucination is a form of vikalpa, as well. I knew a very skillful liar who occasionally had hallucinations so strong that those around him had to go along with it to keep him from going completely over the edge. One time he kept seeing flowers in the air and demanding of me what their "message" was. It was taxing on many levels, believe me. The only good thing was that when the hallucinations ended he would not remember having them, so when it was over it was over.

10. That modification of the mind which is based on the absence of any content in it is sleep.

As already pointed out, in the Yoga Sutras nidra refers to dreamless sleep alone, the state in which there is "nothing" in the field of the mind to perceive. Why the term sushupti which specifically means dreamless sleep is not being used is hard to understand. Shankara says that in this sutra nidra definitely does mean sushupti. However it may be, dreaming must be considered by Patanjali to be a form of vikalpa rather than true sleep.

Even though dreamless sleep is "absence of any content" it is not a void, for we remember it. Certainly we perceive it, as Shankara says: "Unless there had been a perception, there could hardly be a recollection. And when one wakes, one does recall, 'I have slept well' and so on. The recollection itself is a reflection of the perception that I have experienced something; unless there had been some experience, that reflection would not be there, nor could there reasonably be any memories about it."

Dreamless sleep is often cited as proof of the witness-Self, for although there is no object of perception, yet something perceives this non-perception. And that something is the spirit whose very nature is consciousness: turiya, the fourth, eternal state of awareness. "Again, a man who has been asleep in an inner room, without any hint from outside however slight, has recollected immediately on waking 'I have slept a long time,' and this would otherwise be inexplicable."

11. Memory [smriti] is not allowing an object which has been experienced to escape.

Memory is both passive and active. Sometimes memories arise without our intending them to, and at other times we intentionally bring them out from our inner mind, usually for a specific purpose. Vyasa says that we are evoking a samskara, an impression always present in the mind. Shankara says: "The perception arises, and then while dying away lays down a samskara in its possessor, the thinker. The samskara corresponds to its cause."

Memory, of course, includes both intellectual and sensory recall. Patanjali, though, is interested only in the intentional act of will that is memory.

12. Their suppression [is brought about] by persistent practice [abhyasa] and non-attachment [vairagya].

Two things are needed for the ending of mental modifications. One is abhyasa–sustained spiritual practice. This is why Krishna speaks of abhyasa yoga in the Gita. The other is purely psychological: vairagya. *A Brief Sanskrit Glossary* defines vairagya as: "Non-attachment; detachment; dispassion; absence of desire; disinterest; or indifference. Indifference towards and disgust for all worldly things and enjoyments."

13. Abhyasa is the effort for being firmly established in that state [of chitta-vritti-nirodha].

Jnaneshwara Bharati expands on this, saying: "Abhyasa means choosing, applying the effort, and doing those actions that bring a stable and tranquil state." Shankara simply says that abhyasa consists of the observance of yama and niyama, which are to be discussed later on.

14. It [abhyasa] becomes firmly grounded on being continued for a long time, without interruption and with reverent devotion.

Vyasa: "Carried through with austerity, with brahmacharya, with knowledge and with faith, in reverence it becomes firmly grounded."

Shankara: "Unless it is for a long time, and unless it is uninterrupted, the practice does not become firmly grounded."

15. The consciousness of perfect mastery [of desires] in the case of one who has ceased to crave for objects, seen or unseen, is vairagya.

Sri Ramakrishna said: "A certain woman said to her husband: 'So-and-so has developed a spirit of great dispassion for the world, but I don't see anything of the sort in you. He has sixteen wives. He is giving them up one by one.' The husband, with a towel on his shoulder, was going to the lake for his bath. He said to his wife: 'You are crazy! He won't be able to give up the world. Is it ever possible to renounce bit by bit? I can renounce. Look! Here I go.' He didn't stop even to settle his household affairs. He left home just as he was, the towel on his shoulder, and went away. That is intense renunciation.

"There is another kind of renunciation, called 'markata vairagya,' 'monkey renunciation.' A man, harrowed by distress at home, puts on an ochre robe and goes away to Benares. For many days he does not send home any news of himself. Then he writes to his people: 'Don't be worried about me. I have got a job here."

Vairagya is not an on-and-off matter, but a permanent cessation of any desire for any object whatsoever. Vyasa says that one with true vairagya "is inwardly aware of the defects in objects by the power of his meditation."

16. That is the highest vairagya in which, on account of the awareness of the purusha, there is cessation of the least desire for the gunas.

The preceding sutra was about vairagya in relation to objects. This goes further and speaks of dispassion-desirelessness in relation to the three modes of prakriti, the gunas. These are discussed at length in the Bhagavad Gita, but simply put they are the three modes of energy behavior or qualities of energy. *A Brief Sanskrit Glossary* defines guna as: "Quality, attribute, or characteristic arising from nature (Prakriti) itself; a mode of energy behavior. As a rule, when 'guna' is used it is in reference to the three qualities of Prakriti, the three modes of energy behavior that are the basic qualities of nature, and which determine the inherent characteristics of all created things. They are: 1) sattwa–purity, light, harmony; 2) rajas–activity, passion; and 3) tamas–dullness, inertia, and ignorance."

There can be attachment to the qualities of subtlety, intelligence, and purity (sattwa), of effectiveness and efficiency and mastery (rajas), and stability and steadiness (tamas). But these, too, are illusory like other objects.

However such vairagya does not come from insight into the nature of objects or gunas but from knowing the Self. Only when we enter fully into the Self will all desire of any kind cease. For that reason Self-knowledge or atmajnana should be our aim at all times, for that alone will eliminate all that stands between us and perfect freedom (moksha or jivanmukti).

17. Samprajñata Samadhi is that which is accompanied by reasoning, reflection, bliss and sense of pure being.

Samprajñata samadhi, also known as savikalpa samadhi, is defined by *A Brief Sanskrit Glossary* as: "State of superconsciousness, with the triad of meditator, meditation and the meditated; lesser samadhi; cognitive samadhi; samadhi of wisdom; meditation with limited external awareness. Savikalpa samadhi." It is a kind of superconscious bridge between relative and absolute consciousness, partaking of both, but neither exclusively. Its distinctive qualities are:

1. The capacity for vitarka–thought and reasoning with sense perception.
2. The capacity for vichara–subtle thought and reflection.
3. Experience of bliss (ananda).
4. Experience of the sense of "I am," "I exist," the sense of individuality of being (asmita).

Vyasa and Shankara consider this sutra as a list of ascending forms of lesser samadhi. Vyasa sums it up: "Of these the first samadhi, with verbal associations, vitarka, is associated with all four [forms]. The second, with subtle associations, vichara, is without the verbal associations of the first. The third, with associations of bliss, ananda, is without the subtle associations of the second. The fourth, being pure I-am, is without the association of bliss. All these samadhis rest on an object." Shankara explains regarding this: "In this sequence of four, an earlier one is associated with the qualities of all the later ones, and a later one is without the qualities of any earlier one."

18. The remnant impression left in the mind on the dropping of the pratyaya after previous practice is the other [i.e., asamprajñata samadhi].

There are two forms of samadhi: samprajñata and asamprajñata. Samprajñata samadhi is characterized by the four qualities listed in the last sutra. When those four are also removed by further practice, then the state of asamprajñata is reached. Jnaneshwara Bharati puts it very well and completely: "The other kind of samadhi is asamprajñata samadhi, and has no object in which attention is absorbed, where only latent impressions [samskaras] remain; attainment of this state is preceded by the constant practice of allowing all of the gross and subtle fluctuations of mind [vrittis] to recede back back into the field from which they arose."

19. Of those who are videhas and prakrtilayas birth is the cause.

Patanjali is now discussing those people who from birth are seen to possess marked psychic faculties and psychic powers, even to a miraculous degree. Such persons are usually assumed to be spiritually advanced and are respected accordingly, but this is not wise. Usually is only because of certain abnormalities in their previous life (or lives) that they now manifest these abilities. Patanjali says that simply being born precipitates these capabilities, and not yoga at all: no, not even in a previous life. He speaks of two classes of such people: videha and prakritilaya.

Videha means "bodiless," and he is referring to persons who for some reason spent much of their time in the previous life separated from their bodies to a great degree. Edgar Cayce, "the sleeping prophet," said that in his previous life he had undergone a lingering death on a battlefield in which his subtle bodies had been almost completely separated from the physical. Dying in that state, when he was reborn he possessed the intense psychic, almost mediumistic, powers he utilized in his later healing work. Spontaneous astral projectors are videhas.

A prakritilaya is a person who in a previous birth has somehow become absorbed into certain psychic levels of existence, the subtle energies of prakriti. Having identified with psychic energies, when they are born they have the ability to access those powers and even work miracles.

Videhas usually manifest intellectual psychic abilities such as intuition, and prakritilayas actually make external changes or produce external phenomena. However, each may overlap into the territory of the other.

The important point Patanjali is making here is that they are NOT spiritually advanced people, but only possessors of unusual abilities, and we must not make the mistake of attributing spiritual wisdom and worth to them. A vivid case was that of Aimee Semple McPherson, the famous evangelist who was a remarkable psychic and healer. She was hailed as a greatly spiritual and even holy person, but in reality she was a drug and sex addict, remarkably unintelligent and amoral, and in the end committed suicide. One time in New Delhi I was visiting with John McDiarmid, head of the UN mission to India. John kept declaring that if he believed "Sister Aimee" had really worked miracles he would stop believing in God, for he knew her true character. Like so many of East and West, John could not distinguish between the psychic and the spiritual. But Patanjali certainly could, and so can we if we apply ourselves.

20. [In the case] of others [upaya-pratyaya yogis] it is preceded by faith [shraddha], energy [virya], memory [smriti] and high intelligence [samadhi-prajña] necessary for samadhi.

Upaya-pratyaya yogis are those that have followed the traditional sequence of yogic practices and disciplines. Their attainments are directly related to (a result of) specific methods. They have not arisen "out of the blue" but have a firm, known basis. Blavatsky often warned her students not to put faith in "natural" psychics who had either been born psychic or had suddenly, spontaneously become psychic. She explained that such persons have no real control over and understanding of their abilities. Further, their abilities could lessen or disappear as mysteriously as they appeared. Instead she advised the students to only consult and have faith in "developed" psychics: those who had become psychic by following specific disciplines and who could keep themselves up to the optimum level through those practices.

The superconscious experience of authentic yogis is preceded and produced by:

1. Shraddha, the faith, confidence, or assurance that arises from personal experience. It can also be based on developed intuition. It may even be faith in a teacher who has been perceived to be trustworthy, faith that stimulates the yogis to practice faithfully. Shraddha can be a factor behind perseverance in yoga practice.
2. Virya is strength, power, energy, and courage. Obviously all these qualities are needed to initiate and maintain yoga sadhana unto its fruition.
3. Smriti is memory or recollection. In this context it means a constant awareness of divine realities, a continual keeping in mind the principles of spiritual life and especially remembering to maintain constant mental practices such as mantra japa.
4. Samadhi-prajna is an interesting hybrid term. Prajna is basically consciousness, but it is also intelligent awareness or wisdom, and even intelligence itself. Samadhi-prajna is all this, but it has

> been produced by samadhi, including the basic spiritual opening states that lead up to full-blown samadhi. Ordinary prajna can be possessed by anyone who has a developed brain and nervous system, but samadhi-prajna is rooted in spirit-consciousness, spirit-intelligence.

I think we can conclude that samadhi is only attained by special people possessing markedly special qualities and abilities. Fortunately, we can all be such special persons, for that is our potential and our destiny. But we must work at it untiringly and constantly. Yogis do not go on vacations any more than God does. "Full steam ahead" is the way.

Vyasa encapsulates it perfectly: "The samadhi resulting from a means [i.e., practice] is for yogis. Faith is a settled clarity of the mind: like a good mother, it protects a yogi. When he has that faith, and is seeking knowledge, there arises in him energy. When energy has arisen in him, his memory stands firm. When memory stands firm, his mind is undisturbed and becomes concentrated in samadhi. To the mind in samadhi comes knowledge by which he knows things as they really are. From practice of these means, and from detachment from the whole field of mental process, arises asamprajñata samadhi."

Then Vyasa writes a kind of preface or introduction for the next sutra:

"Yogis are of nine kinds, according to the methods which they follow, either mild or moderate or intense, and then subdivided according to the energy–mild, moderate or intense–with which they practice these respective methods. A mild method may be practiced with mild or moderate or ardent energy, and so with the moderate method. Of those who practice intense methods,…"

21. It [samadhi] is nearest to those whose desire [for samadhi] is intensely strong.

Vyasa simply says: "They soon attain samadhi and the fruit of samadhi."

Two interesting words are used here: samvega and asannah.

Samvega means intense ardor derived from long practice. So Patanjali is not saying that samadhi is near to those who for some reason or other have an intense desire that is just a flash in the pan. Rather, it is the ripening of the fruit of long practice, practice that has been moving the yogi closer and closer to the goal. It is a matter of magnetism: the closer the object is to the magnet the stronger the pull toward it.

Asannah literally means "sitting near," or near at hand, the implication being that samadhi is always present in potential form, but is "near" only to the ripened yogi who yearns deeply for union with God. It is not at all a matter of mechanical practice, or of a "super yoga" technique. It is in the will of the yogi, for that is the most divine force any of us possesses.

22. A further differentiation [arises)] by reason of the mild, medium and intense [nature of the means employed].

There are three aspects to this: quality and intensity of practice, aspiration, and method. For optimum success we need the maximum amount of actual practice, the most fervent aspiration which impels us to the practice, and the maximum efficiency/effectiveness of the method(s) employed. A mixture of qualities of these three elements are a guarantee of lesser accomplishment. A wise yogi will consider this seriously and continually gauge the quality of these three aspects of his sadhana. Especially he will consider the inherent value of the method(s) employed.

Shankara says: "It is as in the world, where the prize goes to the one who runs fastest in the race." And later Saint Paul said: "Know ye not that they which run in a race run all, but one receiveth the prize? So run, that ye may obtain" (I Corinthians 9:24).

23. Or by total giving of the life to God.

This could legitimately be rendered: "Or by total merging of the life with/into God." This is not a mere: "Here, O Lord, take my life; I give it to you." That is a noble aspiration if intelligent understanding is behind it, but otherwise it is a meaningless sentimental ramble. But

Patanjali is speaking of the actual transformation of life which naturally culminates in union with God.

In the ancient yogic tradition, that of Gorakhnath and the Nath Yogis, the process of transformation is called Samarasya, which means oneness, especially of essence, which results from the elimination of all differences. It is also the process of bringing the human being on all levels into a harmonious resonance with the divine that will automatically result in perfect union with the divine. It is not a making of the yogi into something, but a removal or erasure of all differences (including conflicts) with the Absolute. When this occurs the individual is naturally merged in Brahman and his eternal, divine nature is revealed in that union. This is an extremely important point, for it not only determines the nature of authentic yoga, it reveals nearly all "yoga" to be artificial, and therefore of temporary effect, and ultimately productive of nothing but illusion and illusory change.

It will be helpful to look at some extracts from the book *Philosophy of Gorakhnath* by Askhaya Kumar Banerjea. In fact, I strongly recommend that you obtain a copy of the book and study it carefully, for it reveals aspects of yoga that were virtually unknown until Banerjea did his research and wrote the book.

24. Ishwara is a particular Purusha who is untouched [aparamrishta] by the afflictions of life [kleshas], actions [karma] and the results [vipaka] and impressions [ashayai] produced by these actions.

Ishwara, God, is not a mere conglomerate of all that exists, but is a distinctive Person or Spirit, the sole independent Being on whom all else depends. God is a particular Spirit in the sense that he can be experienced as a definite, definable Being, and even pointed out by the masters of wisdom.

Part of his uniqueness is the fact that he "touches" and rules all things, but is absolutely untouched by anything. (The Bhagavad Gita emphasizes this, especially.) Although the source of existence and action, Ishwara transcends them and is therefore untouched/unaffected by the kleshas, the taints or afflictions inherent in relative existence. As already listed, the kleshas are: ignorance, egotism, attractions and repulsions towards objects, and desperate clinging to physical life from the fear of death (Yoga Sutras 2:2-9). No action affects Ishwara in any degree. (Again, see the Gita.)

Nevertheless, Ishwara is intimately connected to all things while remaining separate from them. Ishwara is present in all things as the universal Witness, and is nearer to us than anything can be, for Ishwara is the Self of our Self, the Paramatman within which our Atman exists.

25. In him is the highest limit of omniscience.

This can also be translated: "In him is the unsurpassed seed of omniscience." This is very important, for by perfect union with Ishwara the individual can come to share or participate in his omniscience. That is, the finite can experience the consciousness of the infinite, just as Ishwara already experiences the consciousness of each individual being (jiva). This is a fundamental part of Samarasya–liberation (moksha or mukti).

26. Being unconditioned by time he is guru even of the ancients.

Having existed eternally, Ishwara has been the Guru of all beings, including those exalted primal beings or "gods" whom he made rulers of the worlds. The same with the Manus, the progenitors of the human race. Perhaps the most important point is that he is also the Satguru (the guru who is himself the Sat, the Supreme Reality) of all humanity. We may have human teachers known as upagurus (secondary or subsidiary gurus), but only God can be our Absolute Guru. Unhappily, for centuries the greedy, foolish, and unscrupulous have pretended they were satgurus of other human beings, but that is a shameful fiction.

Since God is eternal, it is from him that all knowledge has come, especially the revelation of spiritual truth. As Vyasa observes in his commentary on the Yoga Sutras: "His purpose is to give grace to living beings, by teaching knowledge and dharma [righteousness].” “There is no other but God to give the teaching which is a boat by which they can cross over the sea of samsara, and he teaches knowledge and dharma to those who take sole refuge in him.... For all the kinds of knowledge arise from him, as sparks of fire from a blaze or drops of water from the sea,” says Shankara, commenting on Vyasa's words. Therefore Patanjali concludes: “Being unconditioned by time he is Guru even of the Ancients.”

Dwelling in the hearts of all, God continues to be the Guru of questing souls. This does not mean that qualified spiritual teachers are not helpful to us, but ultimately the yogi must be guided by the Divine from within his own consciousness. “The mind is itself guru and disciple: it smiles on itself, and is the cause of its own well-being or ruin,” wrote the great poet-saint Tukaram (*Tukaram's Teachings*, by S. R. Sharma, p. 19). “The mind will eventually turn into your guru,” said Sri Sarada Devi, the consort of Sri Ramakrishna (*The Gospel of the Holy Mother*, p. 340). Swami Brahmananda, the “spiritual son” of Sri Ramakrishna, in speaking about the role of an external guru said: “Know this! There is no greater guru than your own mind. When the mind has been purified by prayer and contemplation it will direct you from within. Even in your daily duties, this inner guru will guide you and will continue to help you until the goal is reached” (*The Eternal Companion*, p. 120).

Therefore Tukaram wrote in one of his hymns: “The guru-disciple relationship is a sign of immaturity” (*Tukaram's Teachings*, p. 20). The fact that Shankara writes in the *Nirvanastakam*: “I am neither guru nor disciple [*gururnaiwa shishya*],” shows that no human being is either guru or disciple in the final analysis, but is a part of the Whole, the only Satguru.

Yogiraj Shyama Charan Lahiri Mahashaya wrote to a student regarding the guru: “No one does anything; all is done by God. The individual [that seems to be the guru] is only an excuse; remain abidingly focused on that Divine Guru; in this is blessing.” And to another: “Guru is the one who is all; Guru is the one who is merciful. You are the Guru within yourself" (*Garland of Letters (Patravali)*, Letters 12 and 45). In *Purana Purusha* by Dr. Ashoke Kumar Chatterjee it is recorded that Yogiraj made these two statements: "I am not a guru. I do not hold the distinction of 'guru' and 'disciple.'" "The Self is the Guru… the immortal, imperishable Guru." Just as Patanjali says that Ishwara (God) is the guru of all, so did Lahiri Mahasaya. Ishwara is identified in Indian thought with the solar power. In his diary Lahiri Mahasaya drew the sun and wrote beside it: "This is the Feet of the Guru." He also wrote: "The Sun is the Form of the Guru."

When Paramhansa Yogananda, who first made Lahiri Mahashaya known in the West, was questioned "about his own role in the religious evolution of this planet," the great yogi replied: "The one Ocean has become all its waves. You should look to the Ocean, not to the little waves protruding on its bosom" (*The Path*, Swami Kriyananda, p. 493). Another time he objected strongly to the suggestion that only his writings should be read in the public services of Self-Realization Fellowship, saying: "I came to make you God-conscious, not Yogananda-conscious." At other times he said: "There is no such thing as 'Yogananda-realization,' only God-realization." To someone who asked about a "disciple," Yogananda replied firmly: "I never speak of people as my disciples. God is the Guru: They are His disciples" (*The Path*, p. 327). Ramana Maharshi particularly emphasized that God is the guru of all, saying: "Only the Supreme Self, which is ever shining in your heart as the reality, is the Sadguru [True Guru]" (*The Power of the Presence,* p. 116).

The supreme example of someone who attained enlightenment without a guru is Buddha, who is referred to in Buddhist texts as "Self-Awakened." All spiritual life is self-initiated from within; we are both guru and disciple as Krishna and Arjuna symbolize in the Bhagavad Gita. Paramhansa Nityananda said: "He [God] is the One guru, the guru Who is in all, the guru of the universe. No [human] person can be your guru, a person can only be secondary. The real guru is Guru of the Universe" (*Chidakasha Gita* 105). To emphasize this, Nityananda never gave initiation or became a guru in any manner or sense, though he was inspirer, guide, and advisor to many.

Neem Karoli Baba was wont to say, "I make devotees [of God], not disciples" (*Divine Reality*, by Ravi Prakash Pande, p. ii.).

Swami Sivananda of Rishikesh used to say: "I abhor gurudom"–the debasing of the student-teacher interaction to a personality cult.

Swami Yatiswarananda, Vice-president of the Ramakrishna Mission, wrote to one of his students: "We really are not gurus. We bring the message of the Guru of gurus. What all service you can get from me you will. But please turn to Him for light and guidance, for peace and blessedness. As you yourself are finding, human beings are not good enough. The Lord, the Guru of gurus, alone can give us the shelter, the illumination and the bliss we need." That sums it up very well.

Another leading spiritual figure of the Ramakrishna Mission, Swami Premeshananda, once wrote: "We have presently become inundated by this 'guru doctrine.' The purpose of the guru is to lead us to the realization of God; but God has been left behind, and the guru has become the latest fashion. So it is not safe to talk about a particular person. If one places a powerful personality before others, they will hold on to him instead of to God."

The aspiring yogi can then feel safe and assured that God will be his guru, just as he has been for all the enlightened throughout the ages.

In conclusion let us look at the words of Sri Ramakrishna himself on the subject as found in the Majumdar translation of *The Gospel of Sri Ramakrishna*: "Satchidananda [Existence-Consciousness-Bliss] alone is the guru; He alone will teach" (1.2.8; also: 4.2.1, 5.1.2, 5.5.1). "If somebody addresses me as a guru I say, 'Away you rascal!' How can I be a guru? There is no other guru except Satchidananda. There is no other refuge but Him. He alone is the ferryman who takes one across the ocean of relative existence" (1.12.8). "A man cannot be a guru" (2.19.6). "He who says of himself that he is a guru is a person of poor understanding" (3.17.4). "The more you will advance, the more you will see that it is He who has become everything and it is He who is doing everything. He alone is the guru and He alone is the spiritual ideal of your choice. He alone is giving jnana, bhakti and everything" (4.26.2). "Do you pray to Satchidananda Guru every morning? Do you?" (4.9.2).

In the Nikhilananda translation, on October 22, 1885, when someone refers to someone as Sri Ramakrishna's disciple, he says: "There is not a fellow under the sun who is my disciple. On the contrary, I am everybody's disciple. All are the children of God. All are His servants. I too am a child of God. I too am His servant. 'Uncle Moon' is every child's uncle!"

Shankara comments: "Just as the human teachers turn their face towards the wholly devoted pupil and give him their favor, so this supreme teacher gives his favor when there is pure contemplation on him."

27. His designator [vachaka] is the Pranava.

Vachaka means that which is denoted by speech, but it can also mean the spoken form of something that has a very real connection with the object of which it is the vachaka, and sometimes is considered the same as the object. "Pranava" means the single-syllable mantra Om in other texts (and many consider it means Om in this verse also), but here it is different, because Patanjali was a Nath Yogi whose sadhana was centered on the sacred mantra Soham. In the Brihadaranyaka Upanishad we find this: "In the beginning this [world] was only the Self [Atman], in the shape of a person. Looking around he saw nothing else than the Self. He first said, I am Soham [*Soham asmi*]" (1:4:1). Ishwara is the "soul" of creation, is immanent in creation, and is the Self of the world, just as we are the Self in our body. So the first thing Ishwara did at the beginning of creation was to "speak" himself as the word Soham, saying, "I am Soham." Therefore the consciousness of the Self is called Soham Bhava, the consciousness of Soham: I Am That. (See *Soham Yoga, The Yoga of the Self.*)

So the vachaka of Ishwara is Soham. But it is our vachaka also. Therefore:

28. Its constant repetition and meditation on its meaning [is the way].

The japa (repetition) and meditation of Soham together are the way to liberation.

29. From it [result] the disappearance of obstacles [to enlightenment] and turning inward of consciousness.

This is quite clear. Now Patanjali enumerates the obstacles and their effects on us.

30. Disease [vyadhi], languor [styana], doubt [samshaya], carelessness [pramada], laziness [alasya], worldly-mindedness [avirati], delusion [bhranti-darshana], non-achievement of a stage [alabdhabhumikatva], instability [anavashtitatvani], these (nine) cause the distraction of the mind and they are the obstacles [to yoga].

These are too important to not look at closely. After the definition of each I will give I. K. Taimni's comments from *The Science of Yoga.*

Vyadhi: Disease of the body. "This is obviously a hindrance in the path of the Yogi because it draws the mind again and again to the physical body and makes it difficult to keep it directed inwards."

Styana: Dullness; languor, debility; drooping state. "Some people have an apparently healthy physical body but lack nerve power so that they always feel below par and disinclined to take up any work requiring prolonged exertion. This chronic fatigue is in many cases psychological in origin and due to the absence of any definite and dynamic purpose in life. In other cases it is due to some defect in the Pranamaya Kosha which results in an inadequate supply of vital force to the physical body. Whatever its cause it acts as an obstacle because it undermines all efforts to practice Sadhana."

Samshaya: Doubt; suspicion. "An unshakeable faith in the efficacy of Yoga and its methods is a *sine qua non* for its successful practice. Such faith is needed in achieving success in any line of endeavor but more so in this line because of the peculiar conditions under which the Yogi has to work. In the Divine adventure which he has undertaken the objective is unknown and there are no clearly defined standards by which he can judge and measure his progress. Doubts of various kinds are therefore liable to arise in his mind. Is there really any Reality to be realized or is he merely pursuing a mirage? Are the methods he is using really effective? Are those methods the right methods for him? Has he the capacity to go through all the obstacles and reach the goal? These and other doubts of a similar nature are liable to assail his mind from time to time especially when he is passing through the periods of depression which come inevitably in the path of every aspirant. It is at these times that he needs Shraddha–unshakeable faith in his objective, in himself and in the methods which he has adopted. It may not be possible to avoid these periods of depression and doubt especially in the early stages but it is his behavior and reaction to them which show whether he has true faith or not. If he can ignore them even though he feels them, he comes out of the shade into the sunshine again and resumes his journey with renewed enthusiasm. If he allows these doubts and moods to interfere with his Sadhana and relaxes his efforts, they acquire an increasing hold on his mind until he is completely side-tracked and abandons the path altogether."

Pramada: Carelessness; fault; guilt. "This is another obstacle which besets the path of many aspirants for the Yogic life. It has the effect of relaxing the mind and thus undermines its concentration. Some people are careless by nature and when they come into the field of Yoga they bring their carelessness with them. Carelessness is a weakness which prevents a man from achieving eminence in any line of endeavor and condemns him to a mediocre life. But in the field of Yoga it is not only an obstacle but a great danger and the careless Yogi is like a child who is allowed to play with dynamite. He is bound to do himself serious injury sooner or later. No one should think of treading this path who has not conquered the habit of carelessness and learnt to pay careful attention not only to important things of life but also to those which are considered unimportant."

Alasya: Laziness; idleness; apathy; sloth. "This is another habit which results in a distracted condition of the mind. Although it results in the same kind of ineffectiveness in life as in the case of languor it is yet different. It is a bad mental habit acquired by continued yielding to the love of comfort and ease and tendency to avoid exertion. If we may say so, languor is a purely physical defect while laziness is generally a purely psychological condition. A restoration to health automatically cures the former but a prolonged discipline based on the execution of hard and difficult tasks is the only means of curing the latter."

Avirati: Hankering after objects; non-dispassion; sensual indulgence; lack of control; non-restraint. "The worldly man is so immersed in the interests pertaining to his outer life that he does not get time even to think about the real problems of life. And there are many people who pass through life without having ever given any serious thought to these problems. When a person takes to the path of Yoga as a result of the dawning of Viveka and of his becoming alive to the illusions of life the momentum of the past is still behind him and it is not so easy to shut out the interests of the worldly life suddenly and completely. These hankerings after the objects of the world still continue to trouble him and cause serious distraction in his mind. Of course, all depends upon the reality of the Viveka. If we really see the illusions which are inherent in the pursuit of worldly objects like wealth, honour, name etc. then we lose all attraction for them and naturally give up their pursuit. But if the Viveka is not real–is of the pseudo-variety–the result of mere 'thinking', then there is constant struggle between the desires which drag the mind outside and the will of the Yogi who tries to make the mind dive within. Thus, worldly-mindedness can be a serious cause of Vikshepa."

Bhranti-darshana: Delusion; erroneous view. "This means taking a thing for what it is not. It is due generally to lack of intelligence and discrimination. A Sadhaka may, for example, begin to see lights and hear sounds of various kinds during his early practices. These things are very spurious and do not mean much and yet there are many Sadhakas who get excited about these trivial experiences and begin to think they have made great progress. Some think that they have reached high states of consciousness or are even foolish enough to think that they have seen God. This incapacity to assess our supernormal experiences at their proper worth is basically due to immaturity of soul and those who cannot distinguish between the essential and non-essential things in spiritual unfoldment find their progress blocked at a very early stage. They tend to get entangled in these spurious experiences of a psychic nature and are soon side-tracked. It is easy to see that the unhealthy excitement which accompanies such undesirable conditions of the mind will cause great distraction and prevent it from diving inwards."

Alabdhabhumikatva: Non-achievement of a stage; inability to find a footing. "The essential technique of Yoga consists, in the earlier stages, in establishing the mind firmly in the stages of Dharana, Dhyana and *Samadhi*, and after *Samadhi* has been attained, in pushing steadily, step by step, into the deeper levels of consciousness. In all these stages change from one state to another is involved and this is brought about by persistent effort of the will. Sometimes this passage is easy and comes after a reasonable amount of effort. At other times the Yogi seems to make no progress and a dead wall appears to be facing him. This failure to obtain a footing in the next stage can cause distraction and disturb the perfect equanimity of the mind unless the Yogi has developed inexhaustible patience and capacity for self-surrender."

Anavashtitatvani: Unsteadiness; instability of mind; inability to find a footing; mental unsteadiness. "Another kind of difficulty arises when the Yogi can get a foothold in the next stage but cannot retain it for long. The mind reverts to its previous stage and a considerable amount of effort has to be put forth in order to regain the foothold. Of course, in all such mental processes reversions of this nature are to a certain extent unavoidable. But it is one thing to lose one's foothold in the next stage because only practice makes perfect and another thing to lose it because of the inherent fickleness of the mind. It is only when the instability is due to the inherent unsteadiness of the mind that Vikshepa can be said to be present and special treatment is called for."

31. [Mental] pain [dukha], despair [daurmanasya], nervousness [angamejayatva] and hard breathing [shvasa-prashvasa] are the symptoms of a distracted condition of mind [vikshepa-sahabhuvah].

Dukha is pain; suffering; misery; sorrow; grief; unhappiness; stress; that which is unsatisfactory.

Daurmanasya is despair, depression etc., caused by mental sickness; feeling of wretchedness and miserableness.

Angamejayatva is shaking of the body; lack of control over the body.

Shvasa-prashvasa is hard breathing; inspiration and expiration. These are the symptoms of a mental state that is outward-turned, impelled toward and absorbed in externalities.

32. For removing these obstacles there [should be] constant practice of one truth or principle.

The meaning of this is so simple that most commentators miss it. Yet both Vyasa and Shankara comment that it means the practice of meditation on the One, and continual awareness of the One outside of meditation. This will unify the mind which is the producer of the problems listed in the previous sutra when it becomes fragmented or scattered by being divided by sensory experience. The only cure for this is unifying the mind by means of meditation. When practiced for a sufficient amount of time, the state of unity can be maintained in the mind even when dealing with the multiplicities of ordinary existence.

The precise manner this is done has just been given us. The One is Ishwara, and Patanjali has told us that his sound-form is Soham and "its japa and meditation is the way," that "from it comes the disappearance of obstacles and the turning inward of consciousness." This is Soham Yoga, Soham Sadhana.

33. The mind becomes clarified by cultivating attitudes of friendliness [maitri], compassion [karuna], gladness [mudita] and indifference [upekshanam] respectively towards happiness [sukha], misery [dukha], virtue [punya] and vice [apunya].

Maitri is friendliness; friendship; love.

Karuna is mercy; compassion; kindness.

Mudita is complacency; joy; happiness, and implies optimism and cheerfulness.

Upeksha[nam] is indifference; equanimity resulting from disinterestedness.

One of the most unfortunate aspects of Western New Thought or New Age philosophy is the idea that the mind is improved by an in-turned "me" kind of cultivation of what the individual wants to see in his mind. But Patanjali tells us that what is needed is a range of positive reactions to others. Further, a positive attitude is to be maintained toward situations as well as people. Of course, these same attitudes should be cultivated toward ourselves, but not exclusively.

Both Vyasa and Shankara insist that indifference must be cultivated toward those they call "habitually unvirtuous." Not ignoring of them as people, but not being affected by their negativity. That does not mean we should accept their wrongdoing as all right, but that we should not allow ourselves to have any emotional or negative reaction to their deeds and habitual character. This also implies that we should not be pestering them and meddling in their lives, trying to "save" or reform them. We should be ready to help them in any way we can, especially by kindness and good will, but basically we must go our way and let them go their way.

Sitting around fuming over the foolishness and evil of others will only create an affinity between us and their faults, and eventually make us like them. As Jesus said: "Follow me; and let the dead bury their dead" (Matthew 8:22). This includes letting the world-involved stew and bubble about the world. As the Sanatkumars said at the beginning of this creation cycle: "What have we to do with all this, we who are intent on knowing the Self?"

(Also known as the Four Kumaras, the Sanatkumars were those advanced souls–Sanaka, Sanandana, Sanatkumara and Sanatsujata–who at the beginning of this creation cycle refused to engage in worldly life despite the command of Brahma. They were then taught by Lord Shiva, in the form of Dakshinamurti, the mysteries of Brahmajnana and attained liberation.)

34. Or by the expiration and retention of breath.

This is one of the sutras that is so simple we are almost sure to miss its meaning–the way Gandalf mistakes "Say 'Friend' and Enter" for "Speak, Friend, and Enter" in *The Lord of the Rings.*

In classical texts on pranayama we find the terms puraka (inhalation), rechaka (exhalation of breath) and kumbhaka (retention or suspension of breath). But they are not in this sutra. Rather, the terms pracchardana and vidharanabhyam are used, and refer to natural, spontaneous movements of the breath, not deliberate working with the breath as in formal pranayama.

To understand this sutra we must remember that the Yoga Sutras begin with a definition of Yoga that involves the chitta and the waves of the chitta. Just as the breeze disturbs the surface of water, in the same way the chitta is disturbed by various things, one of which is breath. And that is why pranayama occupies such an important place in yoga practice. Specifically, the chitta is ruffled by inhalation. Slow inhalation produces the least effect and rapid inhalation produces the most, but there is no form of inhalation that does not produce an effect on the chitta. On the other hand, exhalation does not make waves in the chitta, nor does the suspension of breath, either in or out. Patanjali tells us this to give a complete picture. At this point he is not advocating any particular practice, just giving us information which will help us later on in understanding the nature and effects of actual pranayama.

35. Coming into activity of [higher] senses also becomes helpful in establishing steadiness of the mind.

Translators are divided in their understanding of this sutra. Some consider it to mean that concentrating on any type of sense impression–usually in the form of the memory of such impression, such as visualization–will steady the mind. Others think it means that the arising of the subtle inner senses, especially in meditation, is an aid to steadying the mind. That is why Jnaneshwar says: "The inner concentration on the process of sensory experiencing, done in a way that leads towards higher subtle sense perception: this also leads to stability and tranquility of the mind."

Vyasa and Shankara consider this second view to be the meaning of the sutra. Vyasa says that the yogi must experience inward realities before he can possess full faith in the words of scriptures and teachers: "Therefore some one definite thing has to be directly experienced in confirmation" at least. Shankara says: "For the yogi who is practicing yoga which is to give face-to-face experience, the perception is the first direct awareness, and it gives him confidence, creating enthusiasm for the practice of yoga. It is like the appearance of smoke when wood is being rubbed together to create fire. Such a perception fills him with joy because of the confidence it creates, and brings his mind to steadiness."

36. Also (through) serene [vishoka] or luminous [jyotishmati] (states experienced within).

Vishoka means: blissful; serene; free of grief, suffering or sorrow. Jyotishmati means: effulgence; full of light. Inner experience of a higher level usually consists of one of these two, and sometimes both together. Naturally the mind will become steady when it experiences vishoka states, and the same with jyotishmati experience. Certainly they can be two different kind of states, but most translators, as well as Vyasa and Shankara, consider that Patanjali is speaking of a single experience, which Vyasa and Shankara call buddhi-sattwa: experience of the buddhi in its most subtle level in which the buddhi and the Self are virtually indistinguishable. Actually, they state firmly that the experience of buddhi-sattwa is the experience of I-am (asmita/aham), experience of the Self through the buddhi.

37. Also the mind fixed on those who are free from attachment [vitaraga] (acquires steadiness).

Vitaraga means: free from attachment (raga); one who has abandoned desire/attachment. Such a person is obviously enlightened. However there is a marked disagreement between translators regarding this sutra. Some consider that Patanjali is recommending that the aspirant fix his mind on the abstract ideal of a mind, a mental state, that is free from attachment and yearning/desire. Vyasa and Shankara hold this interpretation, Shankara stating that there must be no external object whatsoever in true meditation. In fact, in his commentary on Sutra 38, Shankara says: "The mind can be caught by the bridle of an object even merely remembered" in meditation. So they definitely do not consider that there should be meditation on an enlightened, liberated being. In fact, Shankara's statement shows that fixing the mind on any form or concept will prevent authentic meditation. (However, the sound form or mantra repeated mentally is not an external object and cannot hinder meditation–just the opposite.)

This demonstrates that the other view–that the yogi should fill his mind with recollection of a person or deity in meditation, either by visualizing a form or simply "thinking about" them discursively–is not correct.

This is not to say that there is no benefit in admiring or even loving a liberated person or divine form, and keeping their depictions in the home (even in the meditation place) and reading about them and even singing their praises. But in doing japa and meditation of their names there should only be fixing of the awareness on the inner, mental mantric intonations. Meditation is a different mode of mind (mentation) altogether, and the distinction must be known and scrupulously maintained.

38. Also [the mind] depending upon the knowledge derived from dreams [swapna] or dreamless sleep [nidra] [will acquire steadiness].

This sutra is all about the insight the person gains by analyzing the dream and deep sleep states.

By pondering the dream state he comes to understand that all experiences of objects are really internal, even in the waking state. (Note that I say the experiences are internal, not the objects.) He also sees that the mind is capable of creating an entire world.

One of my most significant experiences within the first few days after beginning the practice of meditation was a vivid dream in which I was walking along a street with some people and looking at the trees, sky, clouds, buildings, etc. "Look at all this," I remarked to my dream companions, "it is being created by my mind, yet it is so tangible that if challenged I could not prove it is not a waking experience of the concrete world!" I never forgot the wonder I felt at that time. At other times in dreams I have paused and said to myself: "All this is coming out of my mind. How amazing!"

So the yogi comes to realize some very important things: perception is not always objectively real, all perception is internal whether waking or dreaming, and he has the same creative power as God, even if in a limited degree. Also, if he uses the ability to control his dreams, he comes to realize that control of his waking life is possible, that the waking world is also a dream substance, God's dream within which he is dreaming. In time he comes to realize that he needs to awaken into spirit consciousness, leaving the dreams of relative existence behind.

I also well remember how when I was only three or four years old I would stop and ask myself when awake: "Am I really awake, or am I dreaming? Will I dream years and years are passing, only to wake up and find out only a short time has really passed? Could I dream a whole life, only to wake up to find out I am still a little child?" For I had also observed that I could dream a very lengthy dream and find on awakening that only a few minutes had passed. So I knew the sense of time was also illusive and elusive.

The dreamless state opens up even deeper understanding. There is no sensory experience whatever, yet when we awake we are quite aware that we have been asleep and that time has passed. This tells us that in our essential nature we are a witnessing consciousness, that our existence does not depend upon the senses and their objects. We come to understand that we are a conscious spirit. When asked to define the Self, Sri Ramakrishna said very simply: "The witness of the mind."

All this great wisdom can come just from analyzing the dream and dreamless states. Like Sherlock Holmes said, we must not only see, we must observe–and understand.

39. Or by meditation as desired [abhimata].

Most translators interpret this as meaning a person can meditate in whatever manner they desire, or upon whatever object they choose. But if the first were true, then Buddha would not have insisted upon *right* meditation. The mode of practice cannot be at whim. And Shankara again insists that objects should never be dwelt on in meditation. Rather, both he and Vyasa say that previous thought of things that are abhimata (desired; favorite; attractive; agreeable, appealing) trains the mind to be steady, actually teaching it how to be still and intent. So that ability is to be transferred to the Self in meditation.

Of course the sutra may merely mean that the mind is steadied by meditation when the yogi loves the practice itself. Just sitting for meditation appeals to him, so it is easy.

40. His mastery extends from the finest atom to the greatest infinity.

This is not as big a leap as it seems, for it does not mean that after the preceding steps the yogi is master of the cosmos, from smallest to largest.

Rather, it is speaking of the range of the yogi's awareness/concentration. The adept yogi can attune his awareness to perceive the smallest or most subtle objects and also direct his awareness to encompass that which is not only the largest, but also that which is infinite. In other words, under the direction of his will there is no limitation to his awareness.

41. In the case of one whose chitta-vrittis have been almost annihilated, fusion or entire absorption in one another of the cognizer, cognition and cognized is brought about as in the case of a transparent jewel [resting on a colored surface].

The precision of Patanjali is to be noticed and admired. He could have said that the fusion takes place when the modifications of the chitta have ceased, but that is not accurate. The fusion can occur when the modifications have almost come to an end. There is no room for inaccuracy or exaggeration in Yoga.

Patanjali is telling us that when the modifications of the mind-substance are almost eliminated, the yogi is able to completely unite his awareness to his own Self as the knower, the very process and instruments of knowing, and any object that he is perceiving. The Buddhists call this "penetration."

42. Savitarka samadhi is that in which knowledge based only on words, real knowledge and ordinary knowledge based on sense perception or reasoning are present in a mixed state, and the mind alternates between them.

In *A Brief Sanskrit Glossary*, vitarka is defined as: "thought; reasoning; cogitation with sense perception; discussion; debate; logical argument."

Savitarka samadhi is the state of union with an object in which the yogi is able to conceptualize and intellectually define what he is perceiving. He is able to internally analyze and recognize what he perceives. Basically, he can still "think" in that state, though it may not be in the internal verbalization which we usually mean by "thinking." In savitarka samadhi there is not pure, direct knowing that is a divine quality. Rather it is a mixture of intellection and direct perception. However it is the step before nirvitarka samadhi, and its attainment assures the yogi that he is approaching the summit of Kailash.

43. On the clarification of memory [smriti], when the mind loses its essential nature [swarupa], as it were, and the real knowledge of the object alone shines [through the mind] nirvitarka samadhi is attained.

Nirvitarka Samadhi is the state of union with an object in which remembrance of their names and qualities is not present. That is, the mind ceases to be either a perceiver through the outer senses or a thinker in either words or concepts, and becomes so perfect a knower that no distinction can be found in knowing, knower, or known. This is a state of perfect (total) unity in which outer and inner, object and subject, simply no longer exist, literally. I do not mean they are just not present for the yogi, I mean that for him they are no more in the absolute sense.

44. By this [what has been said in the two previous sutras] samadhis of savichara, nirvichara and subtler stages [in sutra 1:17] have also been explained.

Here are the definitions given in *A Brief Sanskrit Glossary*:

Savichara samadhi: A stage in samadhi wherein the mind (chitta) is identified with some subtle object and assumes its form, being aware of what it is and capable of analyzing it by means of the purified buddhi; with deliberation and reasoning or inquiry.

Nirvichara samadhi: A stage in samadhi wherein the mind (chitta) no longer identifies with a subtle object or assumes its form, simply resting in perception without analytical awareness of its nature by means of the buddhi, whose operation has become completely suspended so that only pure awareness remains; without deliberation and reasoning or inquiry.

Nevertheless, only an adept yogi really knows what Patanjali is talking about.

45. The province of samadhi concerned with subtle objects extends up to the alinga stage of the gunas.

In meditation, consciousness is the ultimate object, but our perceptions need to pass through the intervening veils of subtle vibrations between our higher mind, the buddhi, and consciousness itself. Consequently, even though right from the beginning we should be at least dimly aware of the principle of consciousness, nevertheless, we will start to experience the subtle elements (bhutas), the subtle energies of our inner makeup. If the meditation is proceeding as it should, we experience increasingly subtle elements while at the same time our "awareness of awareness" steadily increases. This is the savichara samadhi Patanjali is talking about. Eventually the original state of pradhana (prakriti) is experienced that is beyond the point of differentiation of the three gunas. This is the highest point of savichara samadhi. "Alinga" means without any attribute, characteristic or mark, and in this sutra refers to the undifferentiated prakriti.

Just as the buddhi borders on the Self and reflects the Self, so is this state of samadhi. It is at the apex of experiencing subtle vibration with profoundly experiencing consciousness, for Vyasa says: "There is nothing more subtle beyond pradhana."

46. They (stages corresponding to subtle objects) constitute only samadhi with 'seed'.

Sabija, "with seed," means that which possesses attributes, and produces samskaras or subtle karmas in the experiencer. Sabija samadhi is savikalpa samadhi wherein the seeds of samskaras or karmas are not destroyed, and which produces the highest and subtlest of samskaras or karmas.

47. On attaining the utmost purity of the nirvichara stage (of samadhi) there is the dawning of the spiritual light [adhyatma prasadah].

In contrast to the samadhi spoken of in the prior sutra, nirvichara samadha is nirbija: "without seed," without attributes, and without the production of samskaras or subtle karmas. Nirbija samadhi is nirvikalpa samadhi wherein the seeds of samskaras or karmas are destroyed ("fried" or "roasted") by jnana, and which produces no samskaras or karmas.

When the utmost purity (shuddhasattwa) of the buddhi is attained, then even pradhana in its highest form is transcended and the light of the Self is perceived.

48. There, the consciousness [prajna] is truth-and-right-bearing [ritambhara].

According to *A Brief Sanskrit Glossary*, Ritam is "Truth; Law; Right; Order. The natural order of things, or Cosmic Order/Law. Its root is *ri*, which means 'to rise, to tend upward.'" When a yogi reaches the nirvichara stage his consciousness henceforward reflects the divine order and is oriented solely toward ultimate Reality. Therefore Vyasa comments: "The knowledge which appears in that clearness of the mind in samadhi has the special name of Truth-bearing in the literal sense that it brings truth alone, and there is no trace of erroneous knowledge in it. So it is said: 'By scriptural authority, by inference, and by enthusiasm for meditation practice: in these three ways perfecting his knowledge, he attains the highest yoga.'" Shankara says that the consciousness spoken of in this sutra is born from viveka (discrimination between reality and unreality).

Patanjali's standards must be applied to us first of all, but also to any who claim to have realization of the Truth (Sat).

49. The knowledge based on inference or testimony is different from direct knowledge obtained in the higher states of consciousness [see sutra 1:48] because it is confined to a particular object [or aspect].

That is, such knowledge is only relative and limited to one object at a time, whereas the knowing in samadhi is absolute, unlimited, and all-inclusive, for Brahman is described as "That which when known, all becomes known."

50. The impression produced by it [sabija samadhi] stands in the way of other impressions.

Vyasa explains this perfectly, saying: "The samskara produced by truth-bearing knowledge removes the accumulated deposit of samskaras of extraversion. When the extravertive samskaras are overcome, no ideas arising from them appear. With inhibition of extravertive ideas, samadhi becomes habitual. Then there is knowledge from that samadhi; from that, more samskaras are laid down of knowledge, and so a fresh deposit of samskaras is built up. From that again knowledge, and from that more samskaras of it." Shankara expands on this, commenting: "Knowledge must set up a samskara. Each time the knowledge is renewed, its special samskara is reinforced. But the renewal of the knowledge is from again taking up meditation on the object, different from itself. It can do this because it is produced by a different object, namely the thing as it really is [yathartha]."

The samskaras produced by sabija samadhi erase the samskaras of ignorance. Vyasa explains this, continuing: "Why would not this new accumulation of samskaras draw the mind into involvement with it? It is because samskaras of knowledge cause the destruction of the taints [kleshas], and so do not constitute anything that would involve the mind. In fact they make the mind cease its activity, for the exertions of mind come to an end in knowledge [khyati]."

This may seem technical, but it is an absolutely practical analysis, for Patanjali intends for us to compare what he says with our meditation experiences and thereby know whether or not we are truly progressing toward enlightenment. In the same way the Bhagavad Gita describes the state of mind of a liberated person in such a way that only the yogi can know whether or not he is in that state. No one can cite the Gita to prove to others that he or someone else is liberated: the individual yogi alone can know the truth of the matter. Both the Gita and the Yoga Darshan are practical manuals of higher consciousness.

51. On suppression of even that owing to suppression of all [modifications of the mind] 'seedless' [nirbija] samadhi [is attained].

From sabija samadhi the yogi passes on to nirbija samadhi, the final step in the liberation of his consciousness. This produces no samskaras and dissolves the samskaras accumulated from sabija samadhi. According to Vyasa: "Thus the samskaras do not cause the mind to continue to exist, but prevent its involvement with anything. The mind, no longer involved, ceased to exists, along with the samskaras which have promoted release. When mind ceases, Purusha abides in his own nature alone, and is therefore called pure, alone, and released."

The section on samadhi (samadhi pada) is now completed.

Sadhana Pada: Yoga Sutras Book II

1. Austerity [tapas], self-study [swadhyaya] and offering of the life [prana] to Ishwara [Ishwarapranidhana] constitute kriya yoga.

First let us define kriya yoga as Patanjali means it.

Because many have read Yogananda's autobiography they assume Patanjali means the method Yogananda named "Kriya Yoga," but this is not at all so. The yoga methods which Yogananda taught in America were never called "Kriya Yoga" before that time, but were always referred to as "the Yoga of Shyama Charan Lahiri" or simply "pranayama." Because the first was awkward to keep saying (or writing) and the second was too general, Yogananda realized the need to give the practice a distinctive name. Since the main effect of all pranayama is purification, he reasonably decided on Kriya Yoga.

(By the way: Since this is so, those Indian teachers who denounce Yogananda as having altered the practice, claiming that they teach "the original Kriya Yoga," are proved by simple historical fact to be false. For if they were really in the traditional line of Indian teachers they would not call it "Kriya Yoga" at all. As my friend Durgaprasad Sahai, a disciple of Swami Keshabananda written about in *Autobiography of a Yogi*, told me: "I practiced that yoga for twenty-five years before I ever heard it called 'Kriya Yoga' in Yogananda's autobiography.")

A Brief Sanskrit Glossary defines "kriya" as: "Purificatory action, practice, exercise, or rite; movement; function; skill. Kriyas purify the body and nervous system as well as the subtle bodies to enable the yogi to reach and hold on to higher levels of consciousness and being." And Kriya Yoga as: "The Yoga of Purification: 'Austerity (tapasya), self-study (swadhyaya), and offering of the life to God (Ishwara pranidhana) are Kriya Yoga' (Yoga Sutras 2:1)." It is this process that Patanjali is speaking about in this and the next sutra.

Kriya Yoga consists of three elements: tapas, swadhyaya, and Ishwarapranidhana. I have written about these in *The Foundations of Yoga*, and will include the relevant sections later on when we are considering yama and niyama, so now brief extracts will suffice.

"Tapas literally means 'to generate heat' in the sense of awakening or stimulating the whole of our being to higher consciousness.... Basically, tapas is spiritual discipline that produces a perceptible result, particularly in the form of purification.... whenever tapas is spoken of it always implies the practice of yoga and the observances that facilitate yoga practice."

"Swadhyaya means 'self-study.' This is usually interpreted as the study of the sacred texts which deal with the nature of the true Self (spirit) and its realization....But it also means keeping a careful watch on the ego-based mind so as to be aware of its delusive and destructive tricks....In swadhyaya we look at and analyze the mind in the calmness and intuition born of meditation."

"Ishwarapranidhana–the offering of one's life to God...is far more on every level than simple religious devotion, and much more than any kind of discipline or self-denial done in the name of spirituality. *It is the giving to God of the yogi's entire life*, not just a giving of material offerings or occasional tidbits of devotion to God, however fervent or sincere."

From a strictly yogic viewpoint we can expand on these a bit. In tapas (meditation) swadhyaya takes place when we become aware of the changes taking place in our mind or see its condition, aspects, characteristics and so forth as we meditate. Also in meditation we are merging our prana, our life energies and breath, with the vishwaprana, the universal life force, and ultimately with Ishwara, their source. So meditation is also Ishwarapranidhana.

2. (Kriya yoga) is practiced for attenuating kleshas and bringing about samadhi.

"Klesha" means taints or afflictions. A klesha is something that diminishes or distorts our consciousness, bringing misery and pain in some form. It also hinders meditation, preventing us from rising to the state of calm, clear concentration and samadhi. Tapas, swadhyaya, and Ishwarapranidhana weaken the kleshas, literally fading them out, washing them away, for they are accretions that have nothing to do with the eternal nature of our Self. Note that diminishing the kleshas is enough to bring about samadhi, which will then itself erase them completely. So we are not facing a herculean task that need daunt us. As Krishna tells Arjuna: "This buddhi yoga taught by Sankhya is now declared to you, so heed. Yoked to this buddhi yoga, you shall avoid the bonds of karma. In this no effort is lost, nor are adverse results produced. Even a little of this dharma protects from great fear" (Bhagavad Gita 2:39-40).

3. The lack of awareness of reality [avidya], the sense of egoism or 'I-am-ness' [asmita], attractions [raga] and repulsions dwesha] towards objects and the strong desire for life [abhinivesha] are the great afflictions or causes of all miseries in life.

Avidya: Ignorance; nescience; unknowing; literally: "to know not." Also called ajnana.

Asmita: I-ness; the sense of "I am;" "I exist;" sense of individuality.

Raga: Attachment/affinity for something, implying a desire for it. This can be emotional (instinctual) or intellectual. It may range from simple liking or preference to intense desire and attraction. Greed; passion.

Dwesha: Aversion/avoidance for something, implying a dislike for it. This can be emotional (instinctual) or intellectual. It may range from simple non-preference to intense repulsion, antipathy and even hatred.

Abhinivesha: Will to live; strong desire; false identification of the Self with the body or mind; an instinctive clinging to life and a dread of death.

4. Avidya is the source of those that are mentioned after it, whether they be in the dormant, attenuated, alternating or expanded condition.

This is why Shankara keeps insisting that jnana alone brings liberation.

5. Avidya is taking the non-eternal [anitya], impure [ashuchi], pain-producing [dukha] and non-Atman [anatman] to be eternal [nitya], pure [shuchi], pleasure-producing [sukha] and Atman respectively.

Anitya: Impermanent; transient.

Ashaucha: Impurity; uncleanness.

Dukha: Pain; suffering; misery; sorrow; grief; unhappiness; stress; that which is unsatisfactory.

Anatman: Not-Self; insentient.

Nitya: Eternal; permanent; unchanging; the ultimate Reality; the eternal Absolute.

Shaucha: Purity; cleanliness.

Sukha: Happiness; ease; joy; happy; pleasant; agreeable.

Atman: The individual spirit or Self that is one with Brahman. The true nature or identity (self).

The whole world is caught in this snare. The yogi must free himself from these illusions right away, even though he must struggle hard against the ignorance and conditionings of many past lives as well as those of this life.

6. Asmita is the identity or blending together, as it were, of the power of consciousness [purusha] with the power of cognition [buddhi].

Having forgotten our true spirit-Self, we have been pulled into the nets of illusion and the false experience that we are the mind and its perceptions. Therefore we say: "I hurt," "I am sick," "I own this," "I lost that," and so forth. We identify with and therefore define ourselves in terms like this. Mistaking the senses and the lower mind for our Self we think and live in an altogether mistaken way, bringing harm and suffering to ourselves, and strive to eliminate the harm and suffering by working with the very things that cause it. So misery and delusion become self-perpetuating. We live our lives like my paternal grandmother drove a car. When my grandfather taught her to drive, at one point she began moving the steering wheel back and forth in rapid, short movements. "What are you doing?" he asked. "I'm giving it more gas!" was her answer.

7. That attraction, which accompanies [results from] pleasure [sukha], is raga.

8. That repulsion which accompanies pain [dukha] is dwesha.

This is the experience of us all, but as Patanjali has pointed out, through ignorance we get sukha and dukha mixed up and our reactions are the opposite of what they should be.

To help us get untangled, a good rule is this: *We cannot become addicted to what is good for us, only to what is bad for us.* We see this in the way people become addicted to alcohol and drugs (including nicotine) that repelled and made them sick the first time they tried them. The body was warning them away, but after some continued use the same body began to demand and "need" them. The body being only an instrument of the mind, the addiction was also psychological.

In the same way unnatural things and behavior become "natural" to us and we blame those who do not see it the same way as we do. In fact, many addicts become very unsettled and even hostile toward those who are not addicted like them, denouncing them as fools or worse. I vividly remember what it was like to be persecuted by a history teacher in high school because I did not smoke cigarettes. It had nothing to do with history, but every so often we would have a class "discussion" on how silly it was to not smoke. (Things have certainly changed!) He would always end up by saying: "In my opinion, people who don't smoke are doing worse things." Such is the evil of addiction.

Many people's favorite foods are the very things that are bad for them to eat. The same is often true of the people they like or "love." Once the mind is distorted it avoids the good and seeks out the bad, sinking into habit patterns that can bind them for lifetimes as they revel in their "free will." As the Gita says: "The man of restraint is awake in what is night for all beings. That in which all beings are awake is night for the sage who truly sees" (2:69).

9. Abhinivesha is the strong desire for life which dominates even the learned.

Abhinivesha is the desperate will to live rising from false identification of the Self with the body; an instinctive and unreasoning clinging to life and a dread of death. Of course it rises from a complete misunderstanding of what life and death really are. Even great yogis can have a subconscious impression (samskara) of this but they can master it. Two examples are given in *Autobiography of a Yogi*.

Lahiri Mahasaya encouraged Sri Yukteswar to attend the *Kumbha Mela* at Allahabad in January, 1894. There he met Mahavatar Babaji. Later, when he met with Lahiri Mahasaya in Benares the following occurred:

> "Gurudeva, the divine master asked me to give you a message. 'Tell Lahiri,' he said, 'that the stored-up power for this life now runs low; it is nearly finished.'
>
> "At my utterance of these enigmatic words, Lahiri Mahasaya's figure trembled as though touched by a lightning current. In

an instant everything about him fell silent; his smiling countenance turned incredibly stern. Like a wooden statue, somber and immovable in its seat, his body became colorless. I was alarmed and bewildered. Never in my life had I seen this joyous soul manifest such awful gravity. The other disciples present stared apprehensively.

"Three hours passed in utter silence. Then Lahiri Mahasaya resumed his natural, cheerful demeanor, and spoke affectionately to each of the chelas. Everyone sighed in relief.

"I realized by my master's reaction that Babaji's message had been an unmistakable signal by which Lahiri Mahasaya understood that his body would soon be untenanted. His awesome silence proved that my guru had instantly controlled his being, cut his last cord of attachment to the material world, and fled to his ever-living identity in Spirit."

When Yogananda returned to India the following conversation took place.

"'Arrangements were recently made for Master to visit Kidderpore [a section of Calcutta], but he failed to go.' Amulaya Babu, a brother disciple, made this remark to me one afternoon; I felt a cold wave of premonition. To my pressing inquiries, Sri Yukteswar only replied, 'I shall go to Kidderpore no more.' For a moment, Master trembled like a frightened child.

"('Attachment to bodily residence, springing up of its own nature [i.e., arising from immemorial roots, past experiences of death],' Patanjali wrote, 'is present in slight degree even in great saints.' In some of his discourses on death, my guru had been wont to add: 'Just as a long-caged bird hesitates to leave its accustomed home when the door is opened.')"

Right identity is the remedy for this dilemma, identity that can be gained only through meditation.

10. These, the subtle ones, can be reduced by resolving them backward into their origin.

11. Their active modifications are to be suppressed by meditation.

In meditation we plumb the depths of the conscious and unconscious mind. There we encounter the subtle energy constructs we call karma and also the energy whorls produced by various experiences in past lives. These are the kleshas. So a great deal of yoga practice is purification and correction of the subtle energies of the mind (manas) and intellect (buddhi).

Naturally we are hoping for meditation to produce amazing and uplifting experiences, but first we have a great deal of simple housekeeping and remodeling to do. The yogi is engaged in a complete reconstruction of the many aspects of his being, in the correction of ages-long distortions and obscurations. It takes a long time and can be tedious, but the healing process always is.

The insight gained in meditation is the basic remedy for the kleshas, which is why in commenting on the first sutra of this Sadhana Pada Shankara states that "yoga practice being the means to right vision [samyagdarshanopaya], comes before right vision. All the yoga methods are means to right vision and therefore precede it in time." First things come first in yoga as well as in all other areas of life. Those who seek the effect before applying the cause can only be disappointed.

Then Shankara tells us: "Right vision is the direct adversary of the kleshas since ignorance is the root of all evil, and ignorance is destroyed when directly confronted by right vision.... the purpose of tapas and the others is samadhi meditation thinning out the kleshas.... Tapas and the others are actions, and as their aim is yoga, they are themselves called yoga. Yoga is the mental state of samadhi, and this yoga of action [kriya] aims at that; he who practices it is a yogi."

Vyasa says: "In one without tapas, yoga does not succeed. Tapas is taught because impurity, colored from time without beginning by karmas, kleshas, samskaras and vasanas, a net of sense contacts, is not destroyed without tapas." Shankara expands on this, saying: "One will not succeed in yoga whose attitude is to cherish the body and bodily things, whose habit is to avoid discomfort of body, senses and mind, and who seek the body absolutely as his self and thinks of it as very delicate. This is why tapas is taught.... Meditation is the mighty opponent of the kleshas."

It is important that we do not think of the kleshas as merely wrong ideas or concepts. They are very real taints of the mind. So regarding the third sutra of this section Shankara writes: "The kleshas are not mental processes. For kleshas are not merely ideas, whereas mental processes are merely ideas. Taints are impurities of the mind, as the disease glaucoma is of the eye. It is from absence of illusion that there is freedom from the impurity of kleshas."

Vyasa sums it all up: "All these kleshas are divisions of ignorance. How so? In all of them, ignorance alone prevails. Whatever is given a form by ignorance, that the kleshas inhere in. They are felt at the time of deluded ideas. When ignorance dwindles, they dwindle accordingly."

12. The reservoir of karmas [karmashaya] which are rooted in the kleshas brings all kinds of experiences in the present and future lives.

A more literal and better translation would be: "Rooted in the kleshas, the karmashaya is experienced in the present and future lives." Equally good would be: "Rooted in the kleshas, the karmashaya is experienced in the seen [drishta] and unseen [adrishta] lives."

The karmashaya is the receptacle or mass of karmas, subtle programmings in the mind, that brings about our present and future lives. Being rooted in in the kleshas, when they are eliminated our karmas vanish right along with them, for the kleshas, too, inhere in the mind.

Though seen and unseen–drishta and adrishta–are nearly always translated interpretively as "present and future," it certainly also means that a great deal of karma manifests in completely unseen areas, such as in the subconscious, and also in our unseen surroundings. For example, if in a previous life we plotted harm to someone but never carried it through and they never knew of it, the same can happen to us, for karma is as exacting as it is demanding. So a lot goes on around and within us that we do not perceive, even though we do see much of the complex, karmic fabric of our lives as it is woven and unrolled in every life. However, subliminally we will pick it all up and process it in the inner mind.

The practical idea being presented by Patanjali is that karma and rebirth are ended when the kleshas are ended.

13. As long as the root is there it must ripen and result in lives of different class, length and experiences.

Jnaneshwara Bharati: "As long as those kleshas remain at the root, three consequences are produced: birth; span of life; and experiences in that life," all in keeping with the character of the karmas involved. Most commenters point out that jati–birth–can also include the kind of species in which we will be born and what "class" within that species will be ours.

14. They have joy or sorrow for their fruit according as their cause is virtue [punya] or vice [apunya].

Punya is merit, virtue, meritorious and virtuous acts, and apunya is the opposite. One brings happiness and the other brings unhappiness. We tend to pick out some object and go after it, thinking that it will bring happiness, but if we are knowledgous and realistic we will instead focus on producing positive karma, for that alone will result in happiness. The pursuit of happiness often ends in the gaining of unhappiness, disappointment, and frustration.

15. To the people who have developed discrimination [viveka] all is misery [dukha] on account of the pains resulting from change [parinama], anxiety [tapa] and tendencies [samskara], as also on account of the conflicts [virodhat] between the functioning of the gunas and the vrittis [of the mind].

When Patanjali says that those who possess intelligent discrimination see that everything is painful (dukha) he does not mean that they go around all glum, cynical, and disgusted, hating everything. Just the opposite: knowing that all is unreal, that Brahman alone is real, they live interiorly in joy. "He whose happiness is within, whose delight is within, whose illumination is within: that yogi, identical in being with Brahman, attains Brahmanirvana" (Bhagavad Gita 5:24). He suffers no pain because he withdraws from that which causes pain. The perspective of such a one is given in Swami Prabhavananda's interpretive translation of this sutra: "But the man of spiritual discrimination regards all these experiences as painful. For even the enjoyment of present pleasure is painful, since we already fear its loss. Past pleasure is painful because renewed cravings arise from the impressions it has left upon the mind. And how can any happiness be lasting if it depends only upon our moods? For these moods are constantly changing, as one or another of the ever-warring gunas seizes control of the mind."

Being changeless in our eternal nature, change (parinama) produces unease and stress in us. I had a highly intelligent friend who was afflicted with a really unfortunate mental trait. Whenever she would be enjoying something, suddenly she would think about how it would end eventually, and the thought would make her miserable for the rest of the time.

Tapa is any kind of unhappiness or distress, marring our peace of mind and causing us to fear the future. This is common to all humanity.

Equally common is virodhat: conflict between our mental state or desires and the way things are in our internal and external life. Many people are at intellectual and emotional war with their life unless they have lapsed into the apathetic hopelessness and "quiet desperation" that characterizes most people. Life is usually miserable or dreary, unless people have sunk even further into a kind of comatose-while-awake condition that is also very prevalent. Most people's lives are not worth living simply because they are not able to live them as they want to. Some people compromise themselves into virtual non-existence.

Commenting on this sutra Shankara flatly states: "Pain is the result of any action." So it really is all dukha.

16. The misery which is not yet come can and is to be avoided.

This is an extremely important sutra because it is implying that all karma can be expunged and never experienced in the future. This is in complete consonance with the view of Shankara that the liberated person (jivanmukta) has absolutely no karma, that so-called prarabdha karma (karma that has become activated and begun to manifest and bear fruit in this life, karmic "seeds" that have begun to "sprout") ceases to exist for the liberated. The present majority view in India is just the opposite, mostly to cover up for the obvious fact that the supposedly enlightened and liberated gurus and yogis of modern times are completely under the sway of karma. So the dogma of the ineradicability of prarabdha is being promulgated. (Two other dodges of reality are "it is just a lila" or "guru is taking on the karma of others.")

The real point is: liberation is the only way to avoid suffering.

17. The cause of that which is to be avoided is the union of the seer and the seen.

"The union of the Seer and the Seen" has already been covered in Sutra 1:4.

18. The seen [drishyam] consists of the elements [bhuta] and sense-organs [indriya], is of the nature of cognition [prakasha], activity [kriya] and stability [sthiti] [sattwa, rajas and tamas] and has for

its purpose [providing the purusha with] experience [bhoga] and liberation [apavarga].

This sutra is a bit tangled in wording, though the meaning is clear. First, here are some definitions to help us:

Drishyam: The seen; the object seen.

Bhuta: The five elementary constituents of the universe.

Indriya: Organ. The five organs of perception (jnanendriyas) are the ear, skin, eye, tongue, and nose. The five organs of action (karmendriyas) are the voice, hand, foot, organ of excretion, and the organ of generation.

Prakasha: Pure Consciousness; cognition.

Kriya: Action; activity.

Sthiti: Steadiness (in this case: inertia).

Bhoga: Experience.

Apavarga: Liberation; release from the bondage of embodiment.

All that is perceptible, both gross and subtle, consist of the three gunas, and exist for the purpose of providing the evolving spirit-consciousness with experience that leads to the ultimate knowledge (vijnana) which produces liberation (moksha). So the drishyam which is an obstacle for the non-yogi is a means to freedom for the yogi.

Harking back to this, commenting on sutra 23 Vyasa observes: "Purusha is the possessor who is joined to his own seen object for the purpose of seeing. Awareness of the seen object, arising from the conjunction, is experience; but awareness of the nature of the Seer is release."

19. The stages of the gunas are the particular, the universal, the differentiated and the undifferentiated.

As we evolve, the energies (gunas) of our makeup progress from the particular to the universal. The personal conditionings of the energies begin to fade away as we move toward our original nature, and we begin to become increasingly in tune with the universe, more at one with it, for creation itself is a bridge to the Infinite. As has been said in the previous sutra, its purpose is our evolution and eventual liberation.

20. The seer is pure consciousness but though pure, appears to see through the mind.

When Sri Ramakrishna was asked to define the Self (atman), he simply replied: "The witness of the mind." No better definition could ever be given; it says it all. The Self witnesses all that the mind does and perceives, and mistakenly believes that it is the doer and perceiver. The mind sees a tree and the Self mistakenly thinks it is the seer, when it is only the witness of the seeing. This is not easy to grasp if we really ponder it and try to figure out all the implications of this fact. The yogi, however, need not approach the matter intellectually but experientially, which makes all the difference. Even so, it takes a great deal of separation from the mind through meditation to really understand the situation, but it does come in time.

21. The very being of the seen is for his sake [i.e. prakriti exists only for his sake].

This has already been covered in sutra 18. However, one new point is introduced. In the Sanskrit text, the word *eva* (only, or alone) is used, meaning that the entire range of relative existence exists solely for the sake of the evolving consciousness; it has no purpose in relation to Brahman. It is not for "lila" (play or sport), nor is it to fill some lack or desire in Brahman (a patent absurdity).

22. Although it becomes non-existent for him whose purpose has been fulfilled it continues to exist for others on account of being common to others [besides him].

Prakriti has two modes: one is universal or cosmic, and the other is individual. Just as the cosmic prakriti is the extension of Brahman the Absolute, in the same way each individual consciousness (atma) has its own prakriti through which it is evolving. When the individual becomes liberated, his prakriti resolves back into consciousness and exists no more as vibration. Merging with him, nothing remains but spirit. However, the other consciousness still possess their own prakriti and continue to experience the cosmic prakriti as well through it.

This would seem pretty obvious, but some people have been egotistic enough to postulate that the universe and other beings exist only in their minds and will cease to exist when they transcend the mind. Others have postulated the same regarding after-death states, teaching that everything experienced after death is nothing but a projection of the individual's mind. In this way they avoid accepting the existence of heavens, hells, and supernatural beings encountered by those who have died and returned to tell about it. "Oh, that was only what he wanted or believed would be there" is their feeble avoidance of reality. This exists in the West in the popular "you make your own heaven or hell right here on earth" of those who fear the possible consequences of immortality. Ostriches may not bury their heads in the sand, but human beings certainly do.

23. The purpose of the coming together of the purusha and prakriti is the gaining by the purusha of the awareness of his true nature and the unfoldment of powers inherent in him and prakriti.

This is an expansion on what has been already said, the new point being that there are powers (shakti) inherent in both the purusha and prakriti that are to be discovered and developed in them. That prakriti has inherent powers is no surprise–it really could not be otherwise–but the idea that there is anything inherent in the individual consciousness (jiva) to be revealed is surprising because consciousness is always just what it is, perfect and unchanging. Nevertheless, in some way experience must affect (but not change) consciousness. For that reason there is discussion of evolving, altering, elevating, or lowering consciousness. The next verse makes everything clear.

24. Its cause is the lack of awareness [avidya–ignorance] of his real nature.

So now we know. Through ignorance the changes in prakriti are attributed to the purusha, and the changes of prakriti are believed to also take part in consciousness as well as in vibratory matter. Consequently:

25. The dissociation of purusha and prakriti brought about by the dispersion of avidya is the real remedy and that is the liberation of the seer.

It has already been stated that ignorance brings about the identity, the seeming contact, of the purusha with prakriti. When avidya is dissolved, illusion is also dispersed, and the purusha is liberated. This is why Shankara continually emphasizes jnana as the sole cure for avidya.

26. The uninterrupted practice of the awareness of the Real is the means of dispersion (of avidya).

Jnaneshwara Bharati: "Clear, distinct, unimpaired discriminative knowledge is the means of liberation from this alliance." Vivekananda: "The means of destruction of ignorance is unbroken practice of discrimination."

Viveka-khyati is not very well translated as "awareness of the Real." Viveka means discrimination between the Real and the unreal, between the Self and the non-Self, between the permanent and the impermanent; right intuitive discrimination; ever-present discrimination between the transient and the permanent. Khyati means apprehension; discernment; knowledge; vision.

So viveka-khyati is the constant awareness-insight into the difference between reality and unreality, between the purusha and the prakriti. And it is not an intellectual exercise, but a state of intelligent illumination resulting from yoga practice, as sutra 28 indicates.

27. In his case the highest stage of enlightenment [prajna] is reached by seven stages.

Vivekananda's explanation of this is extremely valuable:

"When this knowledge comes; it will come, as it were, in seven grades, one after the other; and when one of these begins, we know that we are getting knowledge.

"The first to appear will be that we have known what is to be known. The mind will cease to be dissatisfied. While we are aware of thirsting after knowledge, we begin to seek here and there, wherever we think we can get some truth, and failing to find it we become dissatisfied and seek in a fresh direction. All search is vain, until we begin to perceive that knowledge is within ourselves, that no one can help us, that we must help ourselves. When we begin to practice the power of discrimination, the first sign that we are getting near truth will be that that dissatisfied state will vanish. We shall feel quite sure that we have found the truth, and that it cannot be anything else but the truth. Then we may know that the sun is rising, that the morning is breaking for us, and taking courage, we must persevere until the goal is reached.

"The second grade will be the absence of all pains. It will be impossible for anything in the universe, external or internal, to give us pain.

"The third will be the attainment of full knowledge. Omniscience will be ours.

"The fourth will be the attainment of the end of all duty through discrimination.

"Next will come what is called freedom of the Chitta. We shall realize that all difficulties and struggles, all vacillations of the mind, have fallen down, just as a stone rolls from the mountain top into the valley and never comes up again. The next will be that the Chitta itself will realize that it melts away into its causes whenever we so desire.

"Lastly we shall find that we are established in our Self, that we have been alone throughout the universe, neither body nor mind was ever related, much less joined, to us. They were working their own way, and we, through ignorance, joined ourselves to them. But we have been alone, omnipotent, omnipresent, ever blessed; our own Self was so pure and perfect that we required none else. We required none else to make us happy, for we are happiness itself. We shall find that this knowledge does not depend on anything else; throughout the universe there can be nothing that will not become effulgent before our knowledge. This will be the last state, and the Yogi will become peaceful and calm, never to feel any more pain, never to be again deluded, never to be touched by misery. He will know he is ever blessed, ever perfect, almighty."

28. From the practice of the component exercises of yoga, on the destruction of impurity, arises spiritual illumination [jnana] which develops into awareness of Reality [viveka].

Jnaneshwar Bharati: "Through the practice of the different limbs, or steps to Yoga, whereby impurities are eliminated, there arises an illumination that culminates in discriminative wisdom, or enlightenment."

It is necessary for us to understand that mere practice of the mechanics of yoga will not lead to enlightenment, that the prerequisites of yama and niyama, the "ten commandments of yoga," as well as the adoption of all aspects of dharma must also be there. It is like growing plants. The plants grow from seeds, but if the soil is not of the right character and if there is no moisture or sunlight, even the best of seeds will not germinate and grow into the desired plant. Vyasa and Shankara insist on this, pointing out that both yoga practice and dharma together are what produces enlightenment.

29. Self-restraints [yama], fixed observances [niyama], posture [asana], regulation of breath [pranayama], abstraction [pratyahara],

concentration [dharana], contemplation [dhyana], trance [samadhi] are the eight parts (of the self-discipline of Yoga).

These eight "limbs" (angas) of yoga will now be considered in detail. I will be presenting sections from *The Foundations of Yoga* regarding them.

30. Vows of self-restraint [yama] comprise abstention from violence [ahimsa], falsehood [satya], theft [asteya], incontinence [brahmacharya] and acquisitiveness [aparigraha].

Ahimsa: non-violence, non-injury, harmlessness

In his commentary on the Yoga Sutras, Vyasa begins his exposition of ahimsa: "Ahimsa means in no way and at no time to do injury to any living being." "In no capacity and in no fashion to give injury to any being," says Shankara. This would include injury by word or thought as well as the obvious injury perpetrated by deed, for Shankara comments: "Ahimsa is to be practiced in every capacity: body, speech, and mind."

Even a simple understanding of the law of karma enables us to realize the terrible consequences of murder for the murderer. As Vyasa explains: "The killer deprives the victim of spirit, hurts him with a blow of a weapon, and then tears him away from life. Because he has deprived another of spirit, the supports of his own life, animate or inanimate, become weakened. Because he has caused pain, he experiences pain himself.... Because he has torn another from life, he goes to live in a life in which every moment he wishes to die, because the retribution as pain has to work itself right out, while he is panting for death."

Ahimsa is not willfully causing any harm or pain whatsoever to any being whatsoever, in any degree whatsoever. Ahimsa includes strict abstinence from any form of injury in act, speech, or thought. All forms of violence–verbal or physical, causing mental injury or pain, and angry or malicious damage or misuse of physical objects–are violations of ahimsa, unthinkable for the yogi.

Vyasa immediately points out that all the other abstinences and observances, yama and niyama, are really rooted in ahimsa, for they involve preventing harm to ourselves and to others through negative action or the neglect of positive action: "The other niyamas and yamas are rooted in this, and they are practiced only to bring this to its culmination, only for perfecting this. They are taught only as means to bring this out in its purity. For so it is said: 'Whatever many vows the man of Brahman [God] would undertake, only in so far as he thereby refrains from doing harm impelled by delusion, does he bring out ahimsa in its purity.'" And Shankara explains that Vyasa is referring to delusion that is "rooted in violence and causing violence."

In his autobiography Paramhansa Yogananda relates that his guru, Swami Yukteswar Giri, said that ahimsa is absence of the *desire* to injure. In the highest sense ahimsa is a state of mind from which non-injury will naturally proceed. "Ahimsa really denotes an attitude and mode of behavior towards all living creatures based on the recognition of the underlying unity of life," the modern commentator Taimni declares. Shankara remarks that when ahimsa and the others are observed "the cause of one's doing harm becomes inoperative." The ego itself becomes "harmless" by being put into a state of non-function. And meditation dissolves it utterly. But until that interior state is established, we must work backwards from outward to inner, and abstain from all forms of injury.

The aspiring yogi must clearly realize that the observance of ahimsa must include strict abstinence from the eating of animal flesh in any form or degree as well as the use of anything obtained by or derived from the slaughter of animals.

He must do nothing in thought, word, or deed that harms his body, mind, or spirit. On the other hand, he must do whatever benefits the body, mind, and spirit, for their omission is also a form of self-injury, as is the non-observance of any of the yama or niyamas.

Satya: truthfulness, honesty

"Satya is said to be speech and thought in conformity with what has been seen or inferred or heard on authority. The speech spoken to convey one's own experience to others should be not deceitful, nor inaccurate, nor uninformative. It is that uttered for helping all beings. But that uttered to the harm of beings, even if it is what is called truth, when the ultimate aim is merely to injure beings, would not be truth. It would be a wrong." So says Vyasa.

Shankara says that truthfulness means saying what we have truly come to know is the truth, mostly through our own experience or through contact with sources whose reliability we have experienced for ourselves. "Untruthfulness in any form puts us out of harmony with the fundamental law of Truth and creates a kind of mental and emotional strain which prevents us from harmonizing and tranquilizing our mind. Truthfulness has to be practiced by the sadhaka because it is absolutely necessary for the unfoldment of intuition. There is nothing which clouds the intuition and practically stops its functioning as much as untruthfulness in all its forms," says Taimni regarding the most personal and practical aspect of satya.

Bending the truth, either in leaving out part of the truth or in "stacking the deck" to create a false impression, cannot be engaged in by the yogi. Regarding numbers it is said that "figures do not lie, but liars figure." The same is true here. Equally heinous is the intentional mixing of lies and truth. (Some liars tell a lot of truth.) This is particularly true in the manipulative endeavors of advertising, politics, and religion.

Refusing to speak the truth, as well as avoiding speaking or facing the truth, is a form of untruth.

There are many non-verbal forms of lying as well, and some people's entire life is a lie. Therefore we must make sure that our actions reflect the truth. How many people claim to believe in God and spiritual principles, but do not live accordingly? How many people continually swear and express loyalty and yet are betrayers? We must not only speak the truth, we must live it.

Honesty in all our speaking and dealings with others is an essential part of truthfulness. It is absolutely crucial that the yogi make his livelihood only by honest and truthful means. Selling useless or silly things, convincing people that they need them (or even selling them without convincing them), is a serious breach of truthfulness.

Trying to compromise the truth, even a little, making the excuse that "everybody does it" is not legitimate. For "everybody" is bound to the wheel of birth and death *because* they do it. And that is not what we wish for ourselves. We can lie to ourselves, to others, and even to God, but we cannot lie to the cosmos. Karma, the law of cause and effect, will react upon us to our own pain.

It is interesting that Vyasa considers that truthful speech is informative. By that he means that truthful speech is worthwhile, relevant, and practical. To babble mindlessly and grind out verbal trivia is also a form of untruth, even if not objectively false. Nor is foolish speech to anyone's gain. Sometimes also people lie by "snowing" us with a barrage of words intended to deflect us from our inquiries. And nearly all of us who went to college remember the old game of padding out written assignments, giving lots of form but little content in hope of fooling the teachers into thinking the student knew the subject well and was saying something worthwhile or even profound. This is one of today's most lucrative businesses, especially in the advertising world.

Speaking truth to the hurt of others is not really truth, since satya is an extension of ahimsa. For example, a person may be ugly, but to say, "You are ugly" is not a virtue. "What is based on injuring others, even though free from the three defects of speech–not deceitful, nor inaccurate, nor uninformative–does not amount to truth," according to Shankara.

Our intention must never be to hurt in any way, but we must be aware that there are some people who hate the truth in any form and will accuse us of hurting them by our honesty. Such persons especially like to label any truth (or person) they dislike as "harsh," "rigid," "divisive," "negative" "hateful," and so on and on and on. We would have to become dishonest or liars to placate them. So "hurting" or offending them is a consequence of truthfulness that we will have to live with. The bottom line is that truth "is that uttered for helping all beings." For non-injury is not a passive quality, but the positive character of restoration and healing.

Silence can also be a form of untruth, particularly in dealing with the aforementioned truth-haters. For truth is only harmful when "the ultimate aim is merely to injure beings." But if some people put themselves in the way of truth, then they must take responsibility for their reactions to it.

Will Cuppy defined diplomacy as "the fine art of lying." Sadly, it often is. So we must be sure that we do not deceive under the guise of diplomacy or tactfulness.

Self-deception, a favorite with nearly all of us to some degree, must be ruthlessly eliminated if we would be genuinely truthful.

"Therefore let one take care that his speech is for the welfare of all," concludes Shankara.

Asteya: non-stealing, honesty, non-misappropriation

Asteya is abstinence from stealing, which Vyasa defines as: "the improper appropriation to oneself of others' things." He then concludes: "Refusal to do it, in *freedom from desire*, is non-stealing."

What constitutes ordinary stealing is well known to almost all, but human beings have thought up countless ways to steal and not seem to be stealing: all the way from putting slugs in pay telephones to getting people to give us things or money which we neither need nor deserve. Theft and untruth are certainly interrelated. So we must analyze Vyasa's definition and apply it to our situation. But we can consider a few "fudges" that have become respectable and prevalent.

Taking credit that really belongs to another.

Plagiarism, especially in academic matters.

Taking what is not ours, while pretending that we either own it or have it coming to us.

Taking what is not legitimately coming to us, even if freely given. People do this continually in relation to welfare benefits and insurance claims.

Demanding more than a just price or a just wage.

No paying debts, including taxes.

Forcing others to give us something we want from them, whether material or metaphysical.

Not giving to others what we owe them or what we are legally or morally obligated to give.

A lot of people (especially churches and religious groups) expect others to continually give them things or services which they are perfectly capable of paying for. (I am not speaking about unsolicited gifts or charity–that is virtuous.) Or they want big discounts given to them.

Once a natural health practitioner whose financial situation was much worse than mine told me that she was willing to charge only half her usual fee for my treatment, and would even treat me for free if I wanted. I explained to her that since I could afford the full amount it would be stealing from her for me to either accept a discount or free treatment. And I cited the Yoga Sutras in support of my contention. The law applies to *all.*

The prophet Malachi posed the question, "Will a man rob God?" (Malachi 3:8) That is extremely easy to do and extremely common. We all need to ponder that possibility seriously and see if in some way we are doing that very thing.

But all these forms of stealing are inner or outer acts, whereas Vyasa defines non-stealing as essentially a psychological state of "freedom from desire." This, then, is the goal of abstinence from stealing. What must be attained is the state of mind in which there is absolutely no desire or impulse to steal. "Stealing cannot exist in those whose desire has been cut off," says Shankara.

Brahmacharya: continence

"Brahmacharya is restraint of the sex organ and other senses," says Vyasa. From this we see that brahmacharya has a twofold nature: control and continence.

Control: Spirit has two aspects: consciousness and energy. Consciousness is constant, whereas energy is cyclic. It is the movement of energy that produces (and is) our experience of relativity, and it is the development of energy that is the process of evolution. Therefore the conservation and application of energy is the main determinant of success or failure in spiritual endeavor. Diffusion and dissipation of energy always weakens us. Hence brahmacharya is a vital element of Yoga, without which we cannot successfully pursue the greater life of higher consciousness.

Basically, brahmacharya is conservation and mastery of all the energy systems and powers of our being. This is especially true in relation to negative emotions, for tremendous energy is expended through lust, anger, greed, envy, hatred, resentment, depression, fear, obsession, and the rest. Further, they are both the causes and the symptoms of losing self-control, a major aspect of brahmacharya. Research has shown that persons in the grip of these emotions literally breathe out vital elements of the body. For example, the breath of angry people is found to be laden with copper. So negative emotion depletes us physically as well as energetically. Positive emotions on the other hand actually enhance and raise our energy and physical levels. The cultivation of (true) love, compassion, generosity, cheerfulness, friendliness, and suchlike make us stronger and calmer: essential aspects of brahmacharya. It is noteworthy that the word "virtue" is derived from the Latin word *virtus*–power–which in turn is derived from the Sanskrit word *virya*, which means both power and strength.

"A place for everything and everything in its place," is not just a maxim of orderliness. When applied to the individual's energy systems it is the root of strength and health on all levels. Every atom of personal energy possessed by us has both a place and a purpose. To ensure correct placement and expenditure of energy is the essence of the yogic science. And brahmacharya is its foundation.

Continence: Sexuality is usually considered the main focus of brahmacharya because it has such a powerful grip and influence on the human being. It is considered that if sex is mastered, all the senses will be mastered as well. There is simply no way to convince those addicted to and enslaved by sex that continence is supreme wisdom. But a few facts can be meaningful to the sincere seeker.

The life of the senses stifles the life of the spirit by carrying away the discrimination of the intellect, as Krishna says: "When the mind is led about by the wandering senses, it carries away the understanding like the wind carries away a ship on the waters" (Bhagavad Gita 2:67). The basic life-force, the prana, is dissipated through any intense activity of the senses, thus weakening the inner being. But sexual indulgence is incalculably more destructive of consciousness than any other form of sense experience, for it expends the life-force to a degree far, far beyond that of other sense experiences. Both body and mind are depleted through sexual activity.

The Prashna Upanishad concludes: "It is in those who have tapas and brahmacharya that truth is established" (Prashna Upanishad 1:15). The Gita speaks of the worthy yogis as being "firm in the brahmachari's vow" (6:14).

For practical information on brahmacharya the following books are extremely valuable: *WARNING: Sex May Be Hazardous to Your Health* by Dr. Edwin Flatto, *Science Discovers The Physiological Value of Continence* and *Nutritional Sex Control and Rejuvenation* by the great twentieth century Rosicrucian, Dr. Raymond Bernard, *The Practice of Brahmacharya*, by Swami Sivananda, and *The Role of Celibacy in Spiritual Life* by Swami Chidananda.

Aparigraha: non-possessiveness, non-greed, non-selfishness, non-acquisitiveness

Aparigraha includes the ideas of non-possessiveness, non-greed, non-selfishness, and non-acquisitiveness. Vyasa's definition is most practical: "Seeing the defects in objects involved in acquiring them, and defending them, and losing them, and being attached to them, and depriving others of them, one does not take them to himself, and that is aparigraha." Here, as in the other foundations, the true virtue or observance is mostly internal, leading to the correct state of mind for successful yoga practice.

Basically, when a person sees all the effort expended on "things" as well as the unhappiness attendant on both keeping and losing them–what to speak of awareness of their inherent defects–he wisely backs away and frees himself from Thingolatry. Of course we all have to obtain and use many kinds of things, but we can do so objectively, not letting ourselves get stuck up in them like the tar baby of the Uncle Remus story. Being possessed by possessions is truly a great misery; and the belief that happiness comes from external things is truly a great folly.

People do literally lose themselves in "stuff," for they adopt a completely false self-concept. To think that we are what we "have" is to forget who and why we are. Aparigraha clears the inner eye and lets us see our true "face."

It is no simple thing to be a yogi.

31. These (the five vows), not conditioned by class, place, time or occasion and extending to all stages constitute the Great Vow.

Ahimsa, satya, asteya, brahmacharya, and aparigraha are the Great Vow because they require the exercise of will and because of their dynamic effect on us. Even more, they are great because, like the elements, they are self-sufficient, depending on nothing else, and because they cannot be mutated into something else. They are always what they are, and for that reason they are always to be observed with no exceptions whatsoever. They cannot be neglected or omitted for any reason absolutely. Patanjali lists the possible conditions which do affect lesser observances:

class, place, time or occasion, and stages. A brief consideration of each will be helpful.

Class. No one can mitigate or omit the observance of ahimsa, satya, asteya, brahmacharya, and aparigraha because of "who" he "is." In yoga, too, no one is above the law. That is, no one can produce the effects of yama without their observance. I knew an Archbishop with a quick sense of humor. Once he made a pungent remark about someone, and a woman objected, saying, "That remark is not Christian." He simply smiled and replied, "Madam, I do not have to be a Christian–I am an Archbishop!" Though the Archbishop was making a joke, this is an attitude of many, springing from the blindness of egotism.

Place. Whatever may be the ways of a particular place or group of people in which we may find ourselves, the observances of Yama are incumbent upon us. "When in Rome do as the Romans" is one of the silliest axioms ever coined. Peer pressure must never be an influence on us. Nor should unjust rules or laws have any effect on us. What is right must always be done. The will or opinion of others cannot change our obligation to observe the Great Vow. Nor can external conditions change it. Not even to save our lives can we turn from what is forever right.

Time or occasion. Human beings have for some reason always thought that "now" abrogates what was right or true in the past. It does not. Nor does a situation effect any change in what must be done by us as aspirants to yoga. Aversion to being "out of step" or "alienated from society" has no place in the mind and heart of the yogi.

Stage. We never "get beyond" the observance of the Great Vow. Those at the very end of the spiritual journey are as obligated to fulfill the Great Vow as those who are at the beginning. Also, we cannot "go too far" or "overdo" our observance of the Vow. It is all or nothing. "Ahimsa and the others are to be maintained all the time and in all circumstances and in regard to all objects without any conscious lapse," declares Vyasa. Shankara points out that the Great Vow must be observed by us in relation to all beings–not just confined to humans.

Once again we see the psychological nature of the five components of the Great Vow and how their observance is based upon the courage, self-respect, and self-knowledge of the yogi.

32. Purity [shaucha], contentment [santosha], austerity [tapas], self-study [swadhyaya] and self-surrender [ishwarapranidhana] constitute observances [niyama].

Shaucha: purity, cleanliness

Shaucha means purity and cleanliness within the context of attaining unobstructed clarity of consciousness. "The Self, though hidden in all beings, does not shine forth but can be seen by those subtle seers, through their sharp and subtle intelligence" (Katha Upanishad 1:3:12). "He is not grasped by the eye nor even by speech nor by other sense-organs, nor by austerity nor by work, but when one's (intellectual) nature is purified by the light of knowledge then alone he, by meditation, sees Him" (Mundaka Upanishad 3.1.8). "When food is pure, the mind is pure. When the mind is pure, memory becomes firm. When memory [smriti, memory of our eternal spirit-Self] remains firm, there is release from all knots of the heart. To such a one who has his stains wiped away, Bhagavan Sanatkumara shows the further shore of darkness" (Chandogya Upanishad 7:26:2). Which is why Jesus said: "Blessed are the pure in heart: for they shall see God" (Matthew 5:8). And Saint John: "Every man that hath this hope in Him purifieth himself, even as He is pure" (I John 3:2-3). I mentioned before that ahimsa is the motivation behind a vegetarian diet. Some excuse the eating of eggs by saying that no life is taken. That is so. The eating of eggs is not a violation of ahimsa, but it is certainly a violation of shaucha, of purity of diet. And "when food is pure, the mind is pure." Eating the fetus of a chicken is eating a chicken. Sterile eggs are nothing less than chicken abortions. They are impure.

"Internal shaucha is the washing away of the stains of the mind" according to Vyasa. "Shaucha implies purity in seeing and listening…

and washing away the stains of the mind, such as desire and anger, by the waters of meditation," adds Shankara.

Physical cleanliness is important for it eliminates bodily toxins and prevents disease. Inner purification is important for it eliminates mental toxins and prevents inner ills. For the yogi, the most important external aspect of shaucha is purity of diet. This is because the food we eat determines the vibration of our body and our mind. For this reason it is only wisdom to eat a purely vegetarian diet consisting of grains, vegetables, and fruits. (The best information on diet can be found in the books of Dr. Neal Barnard, particularly *Food for Life: How the New Four Food Groups Can Save Your Life.*)

Those who carefully and scrupulously adhere to a vegetarian diet, omitting all meat, fish, and eggs, and avoiding anything that contains them to any degree will perceive how valuable it is to keep such a dietary regimen. (See *Spiritual Benefits of a Vegetarian Diet.*) Not only will their general health improve greatly (assuming that they eat a balanced and nutritious vegetarian diet), they will see how much lighter and intuitive their minds become. A vegetarian diet greatly facilitates the practice of meditation, making very subtle states of consciousness readily attainable and perceptible. Those who have eaten meat, fish, and eggs for a long time may have to wait a while before fully gaining the benefits of vegetarianism, but it will not be long before they begin to see its beneficial effects to some degree.

Vegetarian diet is a crown jewel for the yogi since it embodies the foundations of ahimsa, asteya, aparigraha, shaucha, and tapas and produces purity and clarity of mind and heart.

There is another, far-reaching aspect to shaucha. While discussing the process of evolution, Vyasa and Shankara also speak about the way to infuse ourselves with higher consciousness. They give the simile of terraced fields on a mountainside. The farmer floods the highest field. When it has received enough water, he then breaks the earth barrier between it and the next, lower field, and the water pours down into it and fills it. And so the process goes until all the fields are watered. Vyasa then firmly declares that mere right or good action or external religiosity effect nothing in the way of transformation into a higher grade of consciousness, but that rather it is a matter of the removal of *obstacles* to higher consciousness that is needed. He points out that no effort is needed to get the water into the field–or the higher consciousness into the individual–except that expended in the removal of the barriers. So the secret is to remove whatever blocks the process of evolution, and it will occur as spontaneously as the water pours down into the field.

It is the removal of obstacles that is the highest form of shaucha. To underscore this, Vyasa continues: "Then again, a farmer in his field cannot force the nutrients of water or earth into the roots of his grain. What does he do, then? He removes the obstructing weeds. With these gone, the nutrients enter, of themselves, the roots of the grain." In the same way, when negative karmas, habits, deeds, thoughts, influences, associations, and situations are uprooted from our minds and lives, the higher consciousness and states of evolution will occur naturally. This is exceedingly important for us to keep in mind. For it is purity (shaucha) in this form that enables the divine light to reach us.

Santosha: contentment, peacefulness

Santosha consists of the passive aspect of contentment and peacefulness and the more positive aspect of joy and happiness. Santosha is a fundamentally cheerful attitude based on a harmonious interior condition and an intellectually spiritual outlook. This is possible only through meditation, and is one of the signs of progress in meditation. This must not be equated with mere intellectual "positive thinking" or a forced external "happiness" which is a camouflage, not a real state. Santosha is an inner-based quality that occurs spontaneously. It need not be cultivated or "acted out" any more than the blossoming of a flower.

Santosha is also contentment with simple living, and relates to aparigraha. Vyasa says that "santosha is being satisfied with the resources at hand and so not desiring more." Shankara says: "As a result of the satisfaction with what is at hand, even though there may be some lack, he has the feeling, 'It is enough.'" Santosha is freedom from the "bigger and more is better" syndrome that grips most of us.

Santosha is also the absence of negative emotions and the presence of positive emotions. In its highest form santosha is the contentment and peace that comes from resting in our own spirit.

Tapas: austerity, practical (i.e., result-producing) spiritual discipline

Tapas literally means "to generate heat" in the sense of awakening or stimulating the whole of our being to higher consciousness. It is commonly applied to the practice of spiritual discipline, especially that which involves some form of physical austerity or self-denial. The sages of ancient India were very conversant with the principles of physics and formulated their symbols accordingly. When an object is heated, its molecules begin to move at a faster rate than usual. Thus, tapas is a procedure that causes all the components of the yogi to vibrate at a much higher rate, and to eventually become permanently established in that higher vibration.

Regarding physical tapas Vyasa writes: "Tapas is endurance of the opposites. The opposites are hunger and thirst, heat and cold, standing and sitting, complete silence and merely verbal silence." ("In complete silence, nothing like hand-signs is allowed, whereas in the limited silence, indications by hands, etc., are permitted and it is only actual speech that is banned," according to Shankara.) Shankara says these opposites may occur naturally or by our own choice through self-denial. And both Vyasa and Shankara say that tapas is always done in the light of the capability of the yogi and is never exaggerated, strenuous, or beyond the yogi's natural ability.

Basically, tapas is spiritual discipline that produces a perceptible result, particularly in the form of purification. Tapas is the turning from the unreal to the Real, from darkness to the Light, from death to Immortality.

But it is never a matter of mere thought or desire, it is always *practical action* towards that end. Consequently, whenever tapas is spoken of it always implies the practice of yoga and the observances that facilitate yoga practice.

We are dual in nature: consciousness and energy, spirit and matter. This being so, we need to realize that although we are essentially consciousness (spirit) we are also energy, and therefore we *are* our bodies and our minds. Or rather, we are the conscious intelligence that manifests as our bodies and minds. Our lives need to be lived in this perspective. For example, when we understand this truth we understand why such observances or disciplines as yama, niyama, vegetarianism, and moral conduct are so beneficial and necessary for us.

Swadhyaya: introspective self-study, spiritual study

Swadhyaya means "self-study." This is usually interpreted as the study of the sacred texts which deal with the nature of the true Self (spirit) and its realization. "Swadhyaya is study of works on liberation (moksha)," says Vyasa. "Swadhyaya is study of works on liberation such as the Upanishads," comments Shankara. But it also means keeping a careful watch on the ego-based mind so as to be aware of its delusive and destructive tricks. For it is no external "devil" or "Satan" we need fear, but the "enemy within," the "Dweller at the Threshold" which is our ego-mind complex that has blinded and enslaved us from life to life and has no intention of giving up its domination of us just because we practice a bit of meditation. Therefore we must be wary of its cunning and subtle ways and carefully analyze the debris it casts up into our consciousness in the form of thoughts and emotions. In this way we will see the direction in which it would pull us. We must take our susceptibility to its machinations most seriously. In swadhyaya we look at and analyze the mind in the calmness and intuition born of meditation.

The highest form of self-study is that which is known as *atma vichar*–inquiry into the Self (spirit). We must never let go of the vital question:

Who am I? We must do all we can to find the answer–not from others or from our intellectual ponderings, but by direct experience of ourselves as pure spirit. Taimni puts it this way: "Though swadhyaya begins with intellectual study it must be carried through the progressive stages of reflection, meditation, tapas, etc. to the point where the sadhaka is able to gain all knowledge or devotion from within, by his own efforts. That is the significance of the prefix *swa* (self) in swadhyaya. He leaves all external aids such as books, discourses, etc. and dives into his own mind for everything he needs in his quest."

Ishwarapranidhana: offering of one's life to God

The final foundation, for which all the others are a necessary preparation, is Ishwarapranidhana–the offering of one's life to God. This is far more on every level than simple religious devotion, and much more than any kind of discipline or self-denial done in the name of spirituality. It is the giving to God of the yogi's entire life, not just a giving of material offerings or occasional tidbits of devotion to God, however fervent or sincere. Moreover, as Taimni points out: "The fact that the progressive practice of Ishwarapranidhana can ultimately lead to samadhi shows definitely that it signifies a much deeper process of transformation in the sadhaka than a mere acceptance of whatever experiences and ordeals come to him in the course of his life.... The practice of Ishwarapranidhana therefore begins with the mental assertion 'Not my will but Thy will be done' but it does not end there. There is a steady effort to bring about a continuous recession of consciousness from the level of the personality which is the seat of 'I' consciousness into the consciousness of the Supreme Whose will is working out in the manifest world."

Ishwarapranidhana is total giving. The yogi does not eke out droplets of his life, but pours out his entire life in offering unto God. He gives all that he has, even his very self. And this is only sensible, for the entire aim of yoga is the reunion of the individual spirit with the Supreme Spirit, the falling of the drop into the Immortal Sea. Ishwarapranidhana anticipates this divine union and ensures its accomplishment. This is why the first law-giver, Manu, says that the highest sacrifice (medha) is purushamedha–the sacrifice of the individual spirit.

Ishwarapranidhana is also mentioned in Sutra 1:23, where Patanjali says that the attainment of samadhi is brought near to the yogi "by offering of the life to God." Vyasa comments: "As a result of Ishwara-pranidhana, which is bhakti [devotion and love for God], the Lord bends down to him and rewards him,… and the attainment of samadhi and its fruit is near at hand." Shankara says: "The Lord comes face-to-face with him and gives His grace to the yogi who is fully devoted to Him.… The grace is effortlessly gained through the omnipotence of the Supreme Lord. By that grace of the Lord, samadhi and its fruit are soon attainable."

It is incontrovertible, then, that yoga is a thoroughly theistic endeavor, one which makes God the center of life and its aim, as well.

Taimni has observed in his commentary: "The student will have noticed that in the ideas set forth in the above pages no effort has been made to link up the facts of Yogic philosophy with doctrines which are considered to be religious. But this does not mean that there is no relation between them. In fact, a religious man can see, if he studies the subject of Yoga with an open mind, that all the ideas of Yogic philosophy can be interpreted in religious terms, and the consciousness which the Yogi seeks to uncover within the folds of his mind is nothing but that Supreme Reality which is commonly referred to as God. God is recognized by every religion with any philosophical background to be a Mighty Being whose consciousness transcends the manifested Universe. He is considered to be hidden within every human heart. He is supposed to transcend the mind. Basically, these ideas are the same as those of Yogic philosophy. The main difference lies in the assertion by Yogic philosophy that this Supreme Reality or Consciousness is not merely a matter for speculation or even adoration but can be discovered by following a technique which is as definite and unfailing as the technique of any modern Science. Yoga thus imparts a tremendous significance to religion and places the whole problem of religious life and endeavour on an entirely new basis and it is difficult to understand how any religious man can reject its claims without giving them due consideration."

33. When there is disturbance or oppression by thought [vitarka], the mind should be filled with (or fixed on–bhavanam) that which opposes it [pratipaksha].

Vitarka means thought in the sense of all kinds of intellectual occupation. There is no connotation of either positive or negative thought, but rather intrusive or distracting thoughts whose effect is negative. This includes good thoughts which are harmful if they arise at the wrong time. Pratipaksha means that which opposes, not that which is opposite in character. In other words thoughts of higher things can supplant thoughts of lower things. They need not be specifically opposite in character. Bhavanam means filling the mind with something.

It is a complete misunderstanding to think this verse means that we should bring to mind things of a kind that are seemingly opposite to the character of the thoughts that are cluttering our minds. I say "seemingly" because the dualities or dwandwas, the "pairs of opposites" such as pleasure and pain, hot and cold, light and darkness, gain and loss, victory and defeat, love and hatred, are not two but one, like the two sides of a coin. So thinking of one to counteract the other, such as thinking of generosity to combat selfishness, is worthless, for each are inherent in the other. The same is true even of "good" and "evil." A lot of people positive-think themselves into negative situations. Many people make themselves sicker by affirming they are healthy, because only a sick person makes such an affirmation, and you can't trick the subconscious. Many people pretend to have a superiority complex to cover up their actual inferiority complex.

Patanjali is not telling us to think of opposites, for that is a vitarka too, but rather he wants us to occupy the mind with that which *opposes* thoughts. But what opposes thought? Direct, intuitive experience-insight produced by the practice of yoga and which by its very nature banishes intrusive thought and brings anubhava: "perception; direct personal experience; spiritual experience; intuitive consciousness and knowledge." This is a far cry from the mind-gaming many people think Patanjali is recommending. That is why Jesus asked: "Which of you by taking thought can add one cubit unto his stature?" (Matthew 6:27).

In the seventh chapter of *Autobiography of a Yogi*, Yogananda relates this about Nagendranath Bhaduri, "the levitating saint" and the matter of anubhava:

> "The saint and I entered the meditative state. After an hour, his gentle voice roused me.
>
> "'You go often into the silence, but have you developed *anubhava?*' He was reminding me to love God more than meditation. 'Do not mistake the technique for the Goal.'
>
> "...I continued my after-school pilgrimages to the saint's door. With silent zeal he aided me to attain *anubhava*."

When the mind is filled with buzzing thoughts, japa is the remedy, and when the mind gets distracted by thoughts when meditating, more meditation is the cure.

34. Thoughts [vitarka] of violence [himsa], whether to be done by ones' self or by others, or approved, rising from greed [lobha], anger [krodha], or delusion [moha], either of mild, medium, or intense degree, result in never-ending pain [dukha] and ignorance [ajnana]; thus the mind should be filled with (or fixed on) that which opposes it.

Since ahimsa is the first-mentioned yama, Patanjali uses it as an example, but he is intending for this sutra to apply to all the yamas and niyamas. The important aspect here is that the vitarka, the very thought, of negative deeds, or the rising of negative emotions, must be immediately counteracted by bringing into the mind that which opposes and dispels them. Patanjali also points out that whether contemplating action by ourself, by others, or merely hoped for ("I wish I could...," "somebody ought to...") and approved in the abstract, still it must be squashed instantly. Further, whatever the source, they are to be evicted right away.

Nor can degree determine how we react. We cannot say it was only a mildly negative thought or feeling and therefore of no consequence. Mighty oaks from little acorns grow. Even a hint of violation of yama and niyama must alert us and we must swing into action. Even better, through our japa and meditation we should habitually be in the state of mind (bhava) which will prevent their arising. Preventative medicine is always to be preferred.

There is no end to the pain and darkening of mind that infractions of yama and niyama produce. The only way to end the pain and ignorance is to end the causes. Again, we should seek to live in such a level of consciousness that these negative things cannot arise in the mind. But until then, the artillery must be kept at hand for instant use.

Shankara makes a very bold and bald statement about yoga: "*Success in yoga is determined by result alone...observable by direct perception.*" As the ever-memorable Dr. Bronner used to say: "Judge only by the amazing results."

Patanjali lists siddhis, psychic powers or effects, that result from the perfect observance of yama and niyama. Since yama and niyama deal with the innate powers of the human being, or rather with the abstinence and observance that will develop and release those powers, the manifestation of the development and perfecting of those powers will be automatic.

Before considering the specific siddhis resulting from perfection in yama and niyama, it should be explained that perfection in these virtues means that the ignorance which causes their opposites such as injury, lying, and stealing, has been completely eliminated from the yogi, and also that their reappearance in his thought, speech, or behavior has become absolutely impossible. So perfection (siddhi) in yama and niyama is not a matter of action or inaction but one of perfected consciousness.

35. On being firmly established in non-violence [ahimsa] there is abandonment of hostility in [his] presence.

The eminently desirable nature of this siddhi is evident. Wherever a yogi perfected in ahimsa may be, there no hostility can arise; and if it is already present somewhere, upon the yogi's entry it will cease. The one perfected in ahimsa is a living fulfillment of the following prayer attributed to Saint Francis:

> Lord, make me an instrument of your peace.
> Where there is hatred, let me bring love.
> Where there is offense, let me bring pardon.
> Where there is discord, let me bring union.
> Where there is error, let me bring truth.
> Where there is doubt, let me bring faith.
> Where there is despair, let me bring hope.
> Where there is darkness, let me bring your light.
> Where there is sadness, let me bring joy.
> O Master, let me not seek as much
> to be consoled as to console,
> to be understood as to understand,
> to be loved as to love,
> for it is in giving that one receives,
> it is in self-forgetting that one finds,
> it is in pardoning that one is pardoned,
> it is in dying that one is raised to eternal life.

This was true of Buddha in whose presence hired assassins and even a mad elephant became at peace and incapable of doing harm. "This happens with all living beings," says Vyasa. Many times it has been observed that in the presence of perfected sages wild animals become tame, even friendly, not only toward human beings but even toward their usual enemies or prey. "In the presence of that one who follows ahimsa, even natural enemies like snake and mongoose give up their antagonism," says Shankara. Violent human beings, too, have become peaceful and gentle after contact with holy people in whom ahimsa was completely realized.

36. On being firmly established in truthfulness [satya] the result of action rests on action [of the Yogi] only.

Luckily, we have quite a few authoritative commentaries to elucidate this obscure language. All are unanimous in saying that when the yogi is firmly established in truth in all its aspects, then whatever he says or wills comes about without any action being needed to produce it. As Vyasa explains: "When he says: 'Be righteous,' that man becomes righteous; told by him: 'Do you attain heaven,' that one attains heaven. His word is infallible." "When truth is firm in him, events confirm his words," adds Shankara. Yogananda gives an example of this in the first chapter of his autobiography.

My friend, Sri Abani Lahiri (a relative of Lahiri Mahasaya), told me that his grandfather had the same power even as a child. Once he became angry with another little boy and said, "You should die!" Immediately that boy became deathly ill and was declared by the doctors to have only a few hours of life remaining. When his parents were told, "That Brahmin boy told him to die," they called for him and asked him to tell their son to live. He did so, and the boy was immediately well. Jesus, too, had this power as a child and had to learn how to control it, as recorded in the "apocryphal" gospels. By the power of his word Sri Ramakrishna caused hibiscus blossoms of two different colors to grow on the same plant. At the end of his earthly life, anyone who heard Sri Ramakrishna speak of spiritual awakening became spiritually awakened.

37. On being firmly established in non-stealing [asteya], all kinds of precious things come to him.

Another translation of the second half of the sutra can be: "All kinds of precious things *present themselves* to him." All the treasuries of earth not only are open to someone perfect in asteya, their contents actively seek him out. Yet such a one neither desires nor seeks them. If he did, they would no longer come to him. Precious things may be given by others to those perfected in asteya, or simply appear from the divine hand of Providence. The former Shankaracharya of Joshi Matt, Jagadguru Brahmananda Saraswati, refused to allow anyone to donate money either to himself or to the monastery, whose expenses were great. Yet, he had a box which was always filled with money from which he provided for all the monastery's needs. Yogananda had a little box with a slot in the top where he put in or took out money without counting or keeping record. Yet it was always full. Sri Brahma Chaitanya, a Maharashtrian saint who lived into the twentieth century, was known to be without any resources whatsoever and lived in total frugality. Yet he once made a pilgrimage to Benares where he gave away a tremendous amount of money to the poor and the monastics. As he sat on a simple mat, he kept putting his hand under it and producing the money from an inexhaustible supply. Paramhansa Nityananda literally pulled fortunes in rupees from his kaupin (loincloth) to pay for projects he was supervising. Some yogis can simply reach up in the air and bring down anything they desire.

38. On being firmly established in brahmacharya, vigor [virya] is gained.

Virya is not ordinary physical strength, but an almost supernatural power that manifests as strength of body, mind, and spirit. When through brahmacharya the yogi's normal bodily power is conserved, a marvelous alchemical change takes place, augmenting and transmuting his energies to a level unknown to others. The truth that those who keep their bodily energies intact can accomplish whatever they will has been demonstrated for thousands of years by celibates of all lands and spiritual traditions.

Regarding the brahmachari possessed of virya, Shankara says: "He brings out great qualities without limit from himself. He has irresistible energy for all good undertakings. The sense is, that he cannot be thwarted by any obstacle." See how great spiritual reformers have changed the lives of untold thousands, their influence reaching over the world and lasting even beyond their physical life span. So great is the virya of some saints that their mere touch can heal. Sometimes the clothing they have worn or objects they have touched heal the sick and work other miracles.

Virya also manifests in the brahmachari's words, giving them a power not found in those of others. As Vyasa comments on this sutra: "From the attainment of virya, he draws out invincible good qualities from himself. And when perfected in it, he becomes able to confer knowledge on pupils."

Through the accumulation of virya the powers of the mind develop beyond all bounds. Yogis have often displayed profound knowledge of subjects they had never studied, and on occasion have shown remarkable artistic abilities.

Virya affects the physical body, too. Swami Dayananda, the great Indian spiritual reformer of the nineteenth century, was once mocked by a man to whom he recommended brahmacharya for increase of bodily strength. When the man got into his horse-drawn carriage and told the driver to go on, the chariot would not move. The driver whipped the horses, but to no avail. In disgust and perplexity the man got out of the chariot and discovered Swami Dayananda holding on to its rear axle!

39. On non-possessiveness [aparigraha] being confirmed there arises knowledge of the 'how' and 'wherefore' of existence.

Regarding this Vyasa says: "'What is this birth? How does it take place? What do we become [both in this life and after death], who shall we be and in what circumstances shall we be?' Any such desire of his to know his situation in former, later, and intermediate states is spontaneously gratified." Nothing is more bewildering to the human being than his existence in this world, particularly the how and why of his even being here, no matter how much external philosophy in the form of books or teachers may attempt to answer the gnawing questions set forth by Vyasa.

The reality of the situation is this: until the individual knows for himself by direct perception gained through his own development, life must remain a confusing mystery for him. Since the yogi is attempting to extricate himself from the bonds of birth and death, it is imperative for him to know the why and wherefore of human embodiment in all its aspects. He does not need more theory, however plausible and appealing; he needs to *know*. This knowledge comes from within when all blocks to communication with his inmost consciousness are removed. For this birth has been determined solely by him in his nature as a potentially omniscient and omnipotent spirit. Perfection in non-possessiveness bestows the needed insight. "Since he has no attachment to outer possessions, illumination of the field of his own self appears without effort on his part," explains Shankara.

40. From purity [shaucha] arises disgust for one's own body and disinclination to come in physical contact with others.

This siddhi certainly will not be thought desirable in a body-and-sex-obsessed society that insists on being touched and hugged (and often more) by all and sundry, but the serious yogi should consider it carefully. After all, his intention is to disengage himself from the grinding gears of samsara, the chief of which is body-consciousness. Not only are human beings obsessed with their own bodies, they compound the problem by incessant contact with those of others. This contact results in the confusion and conflict of their personal energies (prana) by the invasion and admixture of other's prana with theirs, particularly their psychic energies. Losing the integrity of their energies in this way, their life force become unbalanced, weakened, damaged, and–yes–defiled. This condition manifests as an endless series of physical, mental, and spiritual ills. "I am not myself" becomes a truism in relation to them. But for those who carefully observe shaucha it becomes otherwise.

"When by practicing purity and seeing the defects in the body, he becomes disgusted with his own body, he becomes free from obsession with the body; seeing what the body essentially is, he has no intercourse with others," writes Vyasa. The disgust for the body spoken of here is not a hatred or an obsessive aversion for the body, but rather a profound disillusionment with the body springing from awareness of its many defects, not the least of which is its unreliability and inevitable mortality. The body is also seen to be a repository of pain, disease and filth, however fine the present momentary outer appearance may be. It is in fact a treasury of death.

"With the ordinary purification of the physical body we become more sensitive and begin to see things in their true light. Cleanliness is mostly a matter of sensitiveness. What is intolerably disgusting to a person of refined nature and habits is hardly noticed by another person whose nature is coarse and insensitive. So this feeling of disgust towards one's own body which develops on its purification means nothing more than that we have become sensitive enough to see things as they really are." So says I. K. Taimni.

41. From mental purity arises purity of the inner nature, cheerfulness, one-pointedness, control of the senses, and fitness for the vision of the self.

Nobody has objection to these, I am sure. When the inner bodies are pure they are refined and fluid, capable of the most subtle practice of yoga and reaching the highest states of consciousness. This state of inner purity is particularly accomplished by thought and diet.

For the inwardly pure there is no need for artificial "positive thinking." Cheerfulness and optimism rise up from within him as a matter of course. And continue arising. Gone forever are mood swings and the "ups and downs" of life. No more valleys or mountaintops: he soars in the sunlit sky of the spirit as naturally as the eagle flies in the air. Whether engaged in outer or inner activity, his mind is intent upon its purpose, no longer scattered or flapping like a flag in the wind. One-pointed meditation becomes effortless for him. No longer does he struggle with the unruly senses and the mind which Krishna says are as hard to control as the wind. (Bhagavad Gita 6:34)

42. From contentment [santosha] he gains unsurpassed [superlative] happiness.

This is because santosha is a state completely free from all desire for objects or the compulsion to gain some outer thing not yet possessed. Such desire is itself great pain, as is usually its fulfillment. Taimni says: "There is a definite reason why superlative happiness abides in a perfectly calm and contented mind. A calm mind is able to reflect within itself the bliss [ananda] which is inherent in our real divine nature. The constant surging of desires prevents this bliss from manifesting itself in the mind. It is only when these desires are eliminated and the mind becomes perfectly calm that we know what true happiness is. This subtle and constant joy which is called *sukha* and which comes from within is independent of external circumstances and is really a reflection of ananda, one of the three fundamental aspects of the self."

Vyasa has this comment: "So it is said: 'Whatever sex pleasure there may be in the world, whatever supreme happiness may be enjoyed in heaven, they cannot be accounted a sixteenth part of the happiness of destruction of craving.'" Simply being without compelling desires is great happiness and peace. Here is how the Taittiriya Upanishad expresses it:

> "Who could live, who could breathe, if that blissful self dwelt not within the lotus of the heart? He it is that gives joy.
>
> "Of what nature is this joy?
>
> "Consider the lot of a young man, noble, well-read, intelligent, strong, healthy, with all the wealth of the world at his command.

Assume that he is happy, and measure his joy as one unit.

"One hundred times that joy is one unit of the joy of Gandharvas.

"One hundred times the joy of Gandharvas is one unit of the joy of celestial Gandharvas.

"One hundred times the joy of celestial Gandharvas is one unit of the joy of the Pitris in their paradise.

"One hundred times the joy of the Pitris in their paradise is one unit of the joy of the Devas.

"One hundred times the joy of the Devas is one unit of the joy of the karma Devas.

"One hundred times the joy of the karma Devas is one unit of the joy of the ruling Devas.

"One hundred times the joy of the ruling Devas is one unit of the joy of Indra.

"One hundred times the joy of Indra is one unit of the joy of Brihaspati.

"One hundred times the joy of Brihaspati is one unit of the joy of Prajapati.

"One hundred times the joy of Prajapati is one unit of the joy of Brahma: but no less joy than Brahma has the seer to whom the self has been revealed, and who is without craving" (Taittiriya Upanishad 2:7-8).

43. Perfection of the sense-organs and body result after destruction of impurity by tapas.

Tapas is like the fire that refines gold through the burning out of all impurities. In relation to the body, tapas removes its limitations and defects. This has been shown by scientific studies:

"Everyone around the water cooler knows that meditation reduces stress. But with the aid of advanced brain-scanning technology, researchers are beginning to show that meditation directly affects the function and structure of the brain, changing it in ways that appear to increase attention span, sharpen focus and improve memory. One recent study found evidence that the daily practice of meditation thickened the parts of the brain's cerebral cortex responsible for decision making, attention and memory. Sara Lazar, a research scientist at Massachusetts General Hospital, presented preliminary results last November that showed that the gray matter of twenty men and women who meditated for just forty minutes a day was thicker than that of people who did not.... What's more, her research suggests that meditation may slow the natural thinning of that section of the cortex that occurs with age." (*How to Get Smarter, One Breath At A Time*, Lisa Takeuchi Cullen. *Time*, January 16, 2006, p. 93.)

"There was a study reported at the American Geriatric Association convention in 1979 involving forty-seven participants whose average age was 52.5 years. It found that people who had been meditating more than seven years were approximately twelve years younger physiologically than those of the same chronological age who were not meditating." (Gabriel Cousens, M.D., *Conscious Eating*, p. 281.)

The process is described by Vyasa as follows: "As tapas becomes complete, it destroys the veiling taint of impurity; when the veiling taint is removed, there are siddhis of the body like the ability to become minute, and siddhis of the senses in such forms as hearing and seeing things which are remote." The body is no longer locked into its habitual patterns of size or location. Nor are the senses any longer limited to functioning within the bounds of proximity of objects. The body and senses become as free as the yogi's spirit, and as expanded in their scope.

44. From self-study [swadhyaya] arises communion with the beloved deity.

This sutra is not speaking of communion with God the Unmanifest Absolute, but with his manifested forms or with powerful beings: gods, realized masters, and others who have evolved beyond the earth plane.

"Gods, sages, and perfect beings to whom he is devoted come before the vision of the man intent on swadhyaya and give him their help," says Vyasa. The help can be in the form of protection, removal of inner or outer obstacles, and even spiritual teaching. His aspiration expressed through swadhyaya and his love and admiration for them of which, through their omnipotence, they are ever aware, draw them to grant him encouragement, assistance, and instruction.

45. Accomplishment of [or success or perfection in] samadhi arises from Ishwarapranidhana.

Though we can define samadhi in many accurate ways, when we think about it we realize that samadhi is totally coming to rest in spirit, the cessation of all else, and the centering of our being in God. Samadhi is entering into the heart of God, into the silence that is the only truth. The perfection of that state is samadhi, which therefore is produced by total devotion of our life to God.

A final word on the subject from Vyasa: "The samadhi of one who has devoted [offered] his whole being to the Lord is perfect.... [By] the knowledge [resulting] from that [samadhi he] knows a thing as it really is."

46. Posture [asana] should be steady and comfortable.

In the Yoga Sutras "asana" does not mean Hatha Yoga postures, but only meditation postures. Asana is both the sitting posture chosen for meditation and steadiness in that posture. It is this second aspect that is meant by Patanjali.

Shankara: "Let him practice a posture in which, when established, his mind and limbs will become steady, and which does not cause discomfort."

47. By relaxation of effort and meditation on the 'Endless' [ananta] posture is mastered.

Jnaneshwar Bharati: "The means of perfecting the posture is that of relaxing or loosening of the effort, and allowing attention to merge with endlessness, or the Infinite."

48. From that no assaults from the pairs of opposites.

Jnaneshwar Bharati: "From the attainment of that perfected posture, there arises an unassailable, unimpeded freedom from suffering due to the pairs of opposites [such as heat and cold, good and bad, or pain and pleasure]."

49. This having been [accomplished] pranayama which is control of inspiration and expiration [follows].

Alice Bailey: "When right posture (asana) has been attained there follows right control of prana and proper inspiration and expiration of the breath."

Satchidananda: "That [firm posture] being acquired, the movements of the inhalation and exhalation should be controlled. This is pranayama."

Vivekananda: "Control of the motion of the exhalation and the inhalation follows after this."

Jnaneshwar Bharati: "Once that perfected posture has been achieved, the slowing or braking of the force behind, and of unregulated movement of inhalation and exhalation is called breath control and expansion of prana (pranayama), which lead to the absence of the awareness of both, and is the fourth of the eight limbs [of yoga]."

I have presented all these translations because it is so common to interpret this sutra as meaning that pranayama is the cessation of breathing, which is not correct, as will be seen.

50. It is in external [bahya], internal [abhyantara] or suppressed [stambha] modification [vrittih]; is regulated by place [desha], time [kala] and number [sankhyabhih], and becomes progressively prolonged [dirgha] and subtle [sukshmah].

Jnaneshwara Bharati: That pranayama has three aspects of external or outward flow (exhalation), internal or inward flow (inhalation), and the third, which is the absence of both during the transition between them, and is known as fixedness, retention, or suspension. These are regulated by place, time, and number, with breath becoming slow and subtle."

Almost every word in this sutra is crucial to a right understanding of pranayama–of the breath phenomena occurring in meditation.

Bahya: External; outward. This means both the breath that is visible by the movement of the body, that is physical, and the process of exhalation.

Abhyantara: Internal; inward. This means the internal breath that is not visible, and also the process of inhalation.

Stambha: Suspended; retention. This is the state of the breath when it is paused, even for a very short length of time. It is not deliberately produced or held, but occurs naturally according to the movement of the subtle prana in the body.

Vritti: Thought-wave; mental modification; mental whirlpool; a ripple in the chitta (mind substance). The breath and mind are one, so any change in the mind produces a change in the breath, and vice versa.

Desha: Place; locus; spot; space. According to the focus of the mind in relation to the body, so will the breath be affected. Also, the breath can be intentionally experience at any point in the body to affect it.

Kala: Time. This is simply how long or short a breath is.

Sankhyabhih: Numbers. Number of breaths.

Dirgha: Long; prolonged; protracted. The breath becomes slow and therefore prolonged during meditation.

Sukshma: Subtle; fine. The breath becomes almost imperceptible physically, but mostly it becomes very internal and is experienced by the yogi as an inner movement more than an outward one. Eventually he perceives that breathing is an act of mind, and therefore all these terms regarding the breath can equally be applied to the mind and its states.

It is usually thought that pranayama is composed of the words *prana* and *yama*, which mean breath (or life-force) and restraint (or control). But it really comes from *prana* (breath) and *ayama*, which means lengthening, expansion, and extension. In meditation the breath becomes subtle, refined, and slow (lengthened, expanded, and extended). "Prolonged and light [subtle]," says Vyasa. Sometimes it is long and slow and sometimes it is slow but short. Whichever it may be, it is always spontaneous and not controlled or even deliberately intended in any way. This is accomplished through objective observation of the breath, and is not an artificial breathing exercise.

51. That Pranayama which goes beyond the sphere of internal and external is the fourth (variety).

Some understand this as the suspension of breath, but Jnaneshwara Bharati says: "The fourth pranayama is that continuous prana which surpasses, is beyond, or behind, those others that operate in the exterior and interior realms or fields." This can be interpreted in two ways:

1) The fourth pranayama is that in which the yogi ceases to be aware of the inhaling and exhaling breath, but clearly perceives the flow of prana which is behind them and which produces them. He follows this internal process and sees it as the true(r) breath.

2) The yogi perceives the perpetual flow of the prana that goes on independently of the breath. Actually, he perceives two distinct flows: inward-outward, upward-downward, yet totally internal and not at all related to the body. They flow simultaneously without interruption within the subtle body, mainly in the sahasrara (astral brain). The physical breath is only incidental in relation to these two movements of the prana. In time they are not just perceived as acts of the mind-substance (chitta) but are seen to be primal concepts within the causal intelligence or karana sharira.

52. From that is dissolved the covering of light.

Jnaneshwara Bharati: "Through that pranayama the veil of karmashaya that covers the inner illumination or light is thinned, diminishes, and vanishes."

In sutra 2:12 we were introduced to the concept of the karmashaya, "the receptacle or mass of karmas; aggregate of works done; latent impressions of action which will eventually fructify," according to *A Brief Sanskrit Glossary*. When the breath is corrected by right practice (and most "pranayama" is very wrong practice, as many saints of India have said, though few pay any attention to them), the karmashaya begins to melt away, for it loses its hold on the subtle bodies that heretofore were in a state of distortion and negative polarity. Just as a magnet attracts metal, in the same way a wrongly-polarized subtle body holds on to the negative impressions of wrong actions, but when its polarity is corrected, those impressions begin to fade out and slip away. With this in mind, Vyasa comments: "It [the fourth pranayama] destroys the karma which covers up knowledge in the yogi who has not practiced pranayama. As it is declared: 'When the ever-bright sattwa is covered over by Indra's net of great illusion, one is impelled to what is not to be done.' By the power of pranayama, the light-veiling karma binding him to the world becomes powerless, and moment by moment is destroyed. So it it has been said: 'There is no tapas higher than pranayama; from it come purification from taints [kleshas] and the light of knowledge [jnana].'" Shankara simply adds: "It is karma by which the light is covered."

53. And the fitness [yogyata] of the mind [manasa] for concentration [dharana].

Jnaneshwar Bharati: "Through these practices and processes of pranayama, which is the fourth of the eight steps, the mind acquires or develops the fitness, qualification, or capability for true concentration [dharana], which is itself the sixth of the steps."

Dharana is defined as: "Concentration of mind; fixing the mind upon a single thing or point. The first sutra of the next book (pada) says: "Dharana is the confining [fixing] of the mind within a point or area" (Yoga Sutras 3:1).

The important point is made by Vyasa in his commentary: "Simply from the practice of pranayama comes the fitness for dharana." No special exercises, specifically aimed at developing the capacity for dharana, are needed. When the breath enters the fourth stage, the mind becomes capable of dharana since the breath and mind are the same and only through that is the mind rendered able to practice dharana, and usually dharana will occur spontaneously at that time.

54. Pratyahara or abstraction is, as it were, the imitation [anukarah] by the senses [indriya] of the mind [chitta swarupa] by withdrawing themselves [asamprayoge] from their objects [vishaya].

This is not a very satisfactory translation of an incredibly difficult verse. Jnaneshwar Bharati says this: "When the mental organs of senses and actions cease to be engaged with the corresponding objects in their mental realm, and assimilate or turn back into the mind-field from which they arose, this is called pratyahara, and is the fifth step." I personally tend to accept his view.

Anukarah means following or imitating. Patanjali says the indriyas follow–or imitate in the sense of taking on the nature (swarupa) of–the chitta. There are two ways to consider what is meant by the indriyas "following" the mind (chitta): 1) The indriyas resolve into the mind-substance itself, having arisen from it. 2) The indriyas go into abeyance and begin passively reflecting objects, just as the chitta does. If this second is the meaning, then pranayama causes both the chitta and the indriyas to enter a state of motionlessness that is yet keenly aware, not deadened or shut down but in total consonance with the pure consciousness of the Self. It is not impossible that together the chitta and indriyas become what yogis call the buddhi. If so, then the buddhi is really more a state of the chitta than a psychic entity.

55. Then follows the greatest [parama] mastery [vasyata] over the senses [indriyas].

Vasyata means mastery in the sense of control or direction. It is the supreme (parama) control because it is control by the Self, not any lesser entity or level. And it is not a control by direct manipulation but of proximity which puts the indriyas into the state of evolutionary perfection. That is, the Self does not make them perfect by acting upon them, but by being in intimate proximity to them. (We cannot say the transcendent Self actually touches anything.) This, of course, is just what the Sankhya philosophy says about the relation of Prakriti to Purusha: Prakriti moves, "lives," and evolves simply because the Purusha is near it, the way fire can make an object hot without touching it.

Vibhuti Pada: Yoga Sutras Book III

1. Concentration [dharana] is the confining [bandhas] of the mind [chittasya] within a limited mental area [object of concentration: desha].

This is not the suppression of the vrittis of the chitta, but rather a fixing of the chitta on a particular place or area, either physical or psychological. That is, the "desha" may be a particular place in the body, such as a chakra, or it may be a visualized image such as a yantra, or a thought, such as a mantra. This mental activity itself produces a vritti. So Patanjali moves to the subject of dhyana in the next sutra.

2. Uninterrupted flow (of the mind) [ekatanata] towards the object [chosen for meditation: tatra pratyaya] is contemplation [dhyana].

Shankara, in his commentary on the Yoga Sutras, says: "A stream of identical vrittis as a unity, a continuity of vrittis not disturbed by intrusion of differing or opposing vrittis, is dhyana." Thus a single-minded production of a stream of identical vrittis, unmixed with any differing vrittis, is meditation as, for example, in uninterrupted repetition of a mantra or awareness of the breath.

3. The same contemplation [tad evarthamatra] when there is consciousness only [nirbhasam] of the object of meditation [swarupa] and not of itself [the mind: shunyam] is samadhi.

We have all experienced being so absorbed in something that we were aware of nothing else but that object, yet we certainly were not in samadhi. (In grade school I used to start reading a book during free time and literally "know nothing" until I would suddenly realize we were in math class.)

The operative word here is *swarupa*, which *A Brief Sanskrit Glossary* defines as: "'Form of the Self.' Natural–true–form; actual or essential nature; essence. A revelatory appearance that makes clear the true nature of some thing." Now that is something very special indeed. It is the knowing of a thing absolutely, comprehending its essential nature and mode of existence. For example, a mantra will become understood completely as an embodiment of a state of consciousness as well as a definite effect on the meditator.

Jnaneshwara Bharati says: "When only the essence of that object, place, or point shines forth in the mind, as if devoid even of its own form, that state of deep absorption is called deep concentration or samadhi." Obviously there will be a vast range in the spiritual character of such objects, so it is a mistake to equate samadhi with Self-realization or even spiritual experience, for from these three verses we can see that a person could experience samadhi on a pebble.

4. The three taken together constitute samyama.

Samyama merely means "combined practice," although Patanjali gives it a definite meaning in the Yoga Sutras. It is a perfect and simultaneous confluence of dharana, dhyana, and samadhi occurring at exactly the same moment. This requires great strength of mind and will.

5. By mastering it [samyama] the light [taj-jayat] of the higher consciousness [prajnalokah].

This is a very dramatic translation and extremely interpretive. All this sutra really says, though remarkable in itself, is that when samyama is attained the realm of direct perception in relation to the object opens to the yogi. As I say, that is itself remarkable, but talk of "higher consciousness" is not so for most objects. "Deeper consciousness" would be a better expression, and that only to the degree that the object of samyama has depth. Again, samyama on a stone is possible. So its nature and character must not be exaggerated and romanticized.

6. Its [Samyama's] use by stages.

"It is applied in stages" is a much more accurate translation, and merely means that one experience of samyama is not enough, but that it must be repeated a few times at least to ensure that the yogi is seeing everything there is to see about the object, as well as to make sure that the yogi's samyama is perfect and not defective or lacking in something. Yoga is no breeze, even in this matter.

7. The three are internal [antarangam] in relation to the preceding ones.

Dhyana is more internal than dharana, and samadhi is more internal than dharana. To truly know something the awareness must increasingly turn within. For the ultimate knowledge is totally internal. "He whose happiness is within, whose delight is within, whose illumination is within: that yogi, identical in being with Brahman, attains Brahmanirvana" (Bhagavad Gita 5:24).

8. Even that [sabija samadhi] is external to the seedless [Nirbija Samadhi: nirbihasya].

All commentators are agreed that this sutra is speaking of the previously described samyama process as being "with seeds" (sabija) rather than "without seeds" (nirbija), and therefore inferior to it. Jnaneshwar Bharati says: "However, these three practices [dharana, dhyana, and samadhi] are external, and not intimate compared to nirbija samadhi, which is samadhi that has no object, nor even a seed object on which there is concentration."

So Patanjali is speaking here of two different realms of experience and consciousness: savikalpa and nirvikalpa samadhi. Savikalpa samadhi purifies and elevates the yogi, but he remains in the realm of relative existence, even though of a high order. Nirvikalpa samadhi takes the yogi beyond relativity into the absolute realm where eventually he will remain forever. (Although I am figuratively speaking of places or realms, Patanjali is meaning it in the sense of states of consciousness alone.)

This may seem a bit beside the point, but Patanjali is preparing us for later sutras which will explain what is attained by various forms of samyama, and he wants us to understand that however amazing the results of the samyama, it will still be in the field of relativity and capable of producing karmic seeds that will keep us in the cycle of rebirth. It is important to know that Patanjali is not recommending these differing forms of samyama, but is wanting us to know how they come about and not to ever confuse them with knowledge of Reality: Brahmajnana.

9. Nirodha parinama is that transformation of the mind in which it becomes progressively permeated by that condition of nirodha which intervenes momentarily between an impression which is disappearing and the impression which is taking its place.

Easily put, and based on the comments and translations of many sages and scholars, this sutra is saying that when someone practices yoga the chitta begins to change. Instead of constantly erupting in vrittis, the number of vrittis begin to lessen. At the same time the awareness begins to increasingly become in-turned rather than out-turned. Eventually, the state of perfect stillness and total inwardness will arise.

10. Its flow becomes tranquil [prashanta] by repeated impression [samskara].

The production of the inward silent state is accomplished by repeated practice which instils it in the mind as a powerful samskara. Jnaneshwara Bharati: "The steady flow of this state [nirodha parinama] continues by the creation of deep impressions [samskaras] from doing the practice."

11. Samadhi transformation [parinama] is the [gradual] settling of the distractions and simultaneous rising of one-pointedness.

This change we desire comes about only gradually as the chitta itself begins to change.

This is important to know because in my yoga pilgrimage I came across some practices that instantly produced samadhi parinama. I was impressed, even at one point telling the one who had taught a certain method to me: "This is the hope of the world." I was wrong! The practice carried with it extremely detrimental side-effects, both physical and psychological. I saw my fellow-practitioners disintegrating in body and mind while being "happy." After a few months I realized that I must stop the practice or get into very deep trouble. Later I met a psychotherapist who told me of patients who had gravely endangered their mental health through that method. He had himself learned it and after only a few sessions with it realized that it had great potential for harm. Other therapists who had investigated it came to the same conclusion.

A psychologist once told me that any drastic and almost instant change in body or mind is always pathological. Time has revealed to me that he was right. So even though yogis can become impatient and wonder: "When will it happen?" the inner world is not one of instant gratification but of steady and permanent change. So for the yogi it is true: Plod Rhymes With God. A teacher of Buddhist meditation, the Venerable Sumana Samanera, said: "First of all, three things are required here: 1. persistence, 2. persistence, 3. persistence. Without great devotion, without extraordinary patience even one who is otherwise gifted will not be able to make progress."

12. Then, again, the condition of the mind in which the 'object' [in the mind] which subsides is always exactly similar to the 'object' which rises [in the next moment] is called ekagrata parinama.

This is an extremely important sutra because nearly everyone thinks that "one-pointedness" is only a condition of the mind and not an experience, which it really is. That is why Shankara defines meditation as "a stream of identical vrittis as a unity, a continuity of vrittis not disturbed by intrusion of differing or opposing vrittis. This is dhyana." And he contrasts the beginning stage of meditation, dharana, with meditation itself, saying: "Whereas in dharana there may be other impressions of peripheral thoughts even though the chitta has been settled on the object of meditation alone–for the chitta is functioning on the location [desha] as a pure mental process–it is not so with dhyana, for there it [the object of meditation] is only the stream of a single vritti untouched by any other vritti of a different kind." It is important to realize that a vritti need not be a thought or an object, but an abstract experience or bhava excluding all other objects or experiences.

13. By this [by what has been said in the last four sutras] the property, character, and condition-transformations in the elements [bhutas] and the sense-organs [indriyas] are also explained.

Sutras nine through twelve explain how changes occur in the elements and sense-organs, and therefore in the chitta. Without this knowledge the aspirant is simply wandering around in a kind of guessing-game rather than being a real yogi.

The Yoga Sutras themselves are a witness to the fact that a person, however sincere, will get nowhere who just learns a technique and nothing else and engages in an unaware, mechanical practice he hopes will eventually benefit him. No authentic yoga teacher simply dispenses methods without instructing the student fully in the rationale and underlying philosophy of the practice. Nor does a worthy teacher fail to instruct the student fully regarding the nature and necessity of yama and niyama, without which he cannot attain any lasting benefit.

14. The substratum [dharmi] is that in which the properties [dharma]–latent [shanta], active [udita] or unmanifest [avyapadeshya]–inhere [anupati].

Usually in Sanskrit texts "dharma" and "dharmi" mean the innate law of righteousness and one who follows that law. But they also mean qualities or characteristics and the substratum in which the qualities and characteristics are seen to manifest or inhere. I would like to include some other translations of this sutra in hopes it will make the meaning a bit more clear.

Pandit Usharbudh Arya: "A dharmi is that which maintains the same attribute throughout the past, present or future, whether that attribute is decreased or increased or lying dormant to become apparent in the future."

Vyas Houston: "The form substratum (dharmi) conforms to the characteristic form, which may be quieted, arisen, and indistinguishable (past, present, future.)"

Jnaneshwara Bharati: "There is an unmanifest, indescribable substratum or existence that is common or contained within all of the other forms or qualities."

Swami Satchidananda: "It is the substratum (Prakriti) that by nature goes through latent, uprising and unmanifested phases."

Alistair Shearer: "Each object carries its past, present and future qualities within it."

The idea set forth here is that all "changes" are not actual changes but the appearance and disappearance of qualities that are inseparably inherent in the essential substance (prakriti or pradhana) of something. Everything exists in a potential state awaiting actualization. Every moment of our existence was inherent in us from the moment we entered into relative existence. We speak of creation going in cycles, but really there is only a revelation of what has been eternally inherent in pradhana. In other words, past, present, and future are just stages in the cosmic motion picture. The screen is the only lasting reality, and that screen is not inert matter, but Consciousness: Brahman. So nothing really ever "goes on" at all except within the perceptions of the jivatman and the Paramatman.

Just as we say: "You can't get blood out of a turnip," in the same way it is impossible to evoke from an object something that is not already there, inherent in it. This is why the Gita says: "One acts according to one's prakriti. Even the wise man does so. Beings follow their own prakriti; what will restraint accomplish?" (Bhagavad Gita 3:33). This has a direct relation to yoga: only that which will invoke or reveal the eternal, inherent nature of the yogi is valid. Many practices produce an effect which will in time vanish, but real yoga is a revelation of what has always been. Only our true nature as consciousness can be permanent and meaningful. This is because only that which has existed forever can continue to exist, and only that state which has been ours from before the beginning, before time came to be, can bring about our liberation. That is why Jesus prayed: "O Father, glorify thou me with thine own self with the glory which I had with thee before the world was" (John 17:5). The Absolute Self, Parabrahman, is our ultimate Self, the glory which we had before the world ever came to exist for us. Therefore that is also our future. Yoga, then, must be focused on the eternal, not on anything lesser. It must deal directly and immediately with our eternal nature as spirit-consciousness. Right from the first it must begin putting us into contact with the transcendent Being which is our own being. We must become more and more aware of what we ARE. Otherwise it is not yoga.

15. The cause of the difference in transformation [parinama] is the difference in the underlying process [krama].

This translation of Taimni is the best I have come across. Vyas Houston renders this sutra: "The separateness of the *krama*-sequintial progression (of each *citta*-field) is the reason for the separateness of *parinama*-transformations." But that itself needs an explanation. Everyone else considers it to mean that different results are gotten from different processes or order of processes applied. This ignores the meaning of krama as the inherent order or sequence of changes that are possible in something. Again, we are dealing with its fundamental composition: the dharmi. Inherent in the dharmi are all possibilities of change. Krama is the divine law or order of things, not some kind of conditioned or dependent sequence or qualities. Again: what is not already present cannot occur. Also, different things have differing krama-sequences. So basically Patanjali is saying that changes are according to the inherent dharma of the dharmi: the krama. There is no such thing as something coming from nothing, therefore what is not eternally present can never appear or come into being. "It is known that the unreal never comes to be, and the real never ceases to be. The certainty of both of these principles is seen by those who see the truth" (Bhagavad Gita 2:16)

When this sutra is pondered we find that it can be applied to just about everything in life, from cooking to caste. Since these are the Yoga Sutras, Patanjali intends for us to explore all its implications for the yogi himself and his yoga methodology and its practice.

One most important thing to realize is that everything is Law. There is no room at all in the order of things (the divine krama) for "grace" or "God's will" in the sense of something that contravenes or obliterates the divine order. Everything goes step by step, and that order is perfect because it is truly divine. Anything else would be disorder and imperfection. Of course krama is itself the grace of Ishwara, the manifestation of his will. So to hope things will get changed around to suit us is not just childish egotism, it is moral idiocy.

16. By performing samyama on the three kinds of transformations [parinama–nirodha, samadhi and ekagrata] knowledge of the past and future.

This section which is known as the Vibhuti Pada, Chapter of Miraculous Powers, is often passed over by teachers because it speaks of the way to acquire various forms of knowledge that do not conduce to atmajnana: Self knowledge. Some think that Patanjali did not write this section since it does not deal with authentic yoga sadhana, but with distracting psychic powers which attract and expand the ego. But it seems to me only reasonable that he would explain how various powers are gained that yogis may mistake for spiritual powers and signs of actual progress in yoga, which they are not. He is warning us against falling into the psychic traps that will confront anyone who is evolving upward.

Certainly the psychic realm is a very dangerous one because both psychic illusions and psychic realities are equally addicting and distracting. We consider this material world to be incredibly hard to overcome and be freed from, but the astral/psychic realms are much harder to escape from because they are usually pleasurable and endlessly fascinating. Being so much vaster than either the physical or causal worlds, and so infinitely complex and interesting, it is possible to wander through those worlds for the duration of many creation cycles, only being somewhat shaken out of their hypnotic fascination at the mahapralaya when they are dissolved around us.

I have known quite a few yogis that became completely enmeshed in the psychic levels and consequently failed to attain any lasting spiritual progress. One of them made millions upon millions of dollars from inventions he discovered through visions received in meditation. That is not the purpose of yoga, but Maya fooled him, repeating the old trick: "All these things will I give thee, if thou wilt fall down and worship me" (Matthew 4:9). Since my friend was a "big fish," Maya snared him with a big net. Who can say what great things he might have done in the world for the liberation of humanity if he had kept his eyes on the one goal instead of wandering off into the byways of technology and material profit. He left his millions behind at death, taking comparatively little advancement with him. This world will surely find him back at some time in the future.

Another problem with this section is its involvement with samyama, the subject of the first four sutras of this pada. The three elements of samyama are listed, but just how to do it is never told. At some time in my yoga sadhana I suddenly knew how to do it; it just came to me when I put my mind to it. It was, as is all real yoga, a purely mental process. I tried it out on a few subjects and each time it worked. I gained a goodly bit of useless knowledge, but found that it really was possible to do what Patanjali says. I never tried out the samyamas that bring psychic powers because I was psychic enough already from previous yoga practice and did not want to run the risk of falling under their spell. I already knew plenty of yogis that had been derailed by psychic powers, some of them disciples of great masters who had taught them better. So I can assure you that samyama is possible, but I have no idea how to instruct you in its practice. And I should not, anyway.

Consequently I am going to only give very brief statements about the results listed in the sutras, and some I will give just as they are with no comment at all.

17. The sound [shabda], the meaning [behind it] and the idea [which is present in the mind at the time] are present together in a confused state. By performing samyama [on the sound] they are resolved and there arises comprehension of the meaning of sounds uttered by any living being.

I know a yogi who was born with a certain degree of this ability. By doing samyama on it he discovered that he had spontaneously developed it in previous lives as a Christian priest through listening to confessions. Since he was only listening, intent on the penitents' words, instead of becoming absorbed in their meaning he became utterly merged in the simple sound of their words, and thereby could read their minds and tell a great deal about their mental and moral character. Jesus referred to the basis of this ability when he said: "Out of the abundance of the heart the mouth speaketh" (Matthew 12:34). The great Eastern Christian mystic, Saint Gregory Palamas, discussed this ability in his writings, commenting that some people are born with it, as was he. Yogananda explains it very well in his commentary on the gospels (*The Second Coming of Christ*). Occasionally this yogi understood what animals were saying to him, as well.

18. By direct perceptions of the impressions [samskaras] a knowledge of the previous birth.

Since samskaras are mental impressions carried over from a previous life, it is possible to recover memories of those lives by concentrating on the individual samskaras. This is perhaps the easiest samyama to do and it reveals the incidents that produced the samskaras. This is the major element of past lives therapy. (It is a mistake to think that only yogis can do these things.)

19. [By direct perception through samyama] of the image occupying the mind, knowledge of the mind of others.

This is a peculiar statement, for it means that by reading the minds of others we come to know what is in their minds. We read their minds by means of reading their minds! Speaking from my own experience I know that if on occasion the dominant impression or projection of a person's conscious mind is picked up by someone, that person can follow it like a thread right back into the other person's mind and come to know them intimately. Frankly, it is an unpleasant and disturbing experience, since most people's minds are cacophonous messes. Further, it is possible to absorb some of their mental vibration and add to our own mental confusion. I knew a yogi who gained that ability during a meditation period. He was meditating with about a hundred people, and his mind began roving from one mind to another. He was so horrified that he forced himself out of meditation, rushed out of the building and went far away from there. After over an hour he became settled in his own mind and went back. But from then on he was on his guard against a repetition of the experience.

20. But not also of other mental factors which support the mental image for that is not the object [of samyama].

Samyama can only be done on the split-second contents of the other person's mental screen, not any other aspects of his mind–at least not as far as the subject of the previous sutra is concerned. (There are many ways to read minds.)

21. By performing samyama on rupa [one of the five tanmatras], on suspension of the receptive power, the contact between the eye [of the observer] and light]from the body] is broken and the body becomes invisible.

The information in this sutra is definitely fragmentary. The yogi I just mentioned told me that he knew of three methods for invisibility, and had experience with one of them. None of them involved samyama on the pure form of the five elements, the tanmatras.

22. From the above can be understood the disappearance of sound, etc.

We can understand if we have both knowledge and experience of these things, but not otherwise.

23. Karma is of two kinds: active and dormant; by performing samyama on them [is gained] knowledge of the time of death; also by [performing samyama on] portents.

Only if a karma that is directly relating to the causation of death is the object of samyama will this work. The same is true with portents that are foreshadowings of karmic operations.

24. [By performing samyama] on friendliness, etc. [comes] strength [of the quality].

This can mean that samyama on a positive quality causes it to be increased and strengthened in the yogi, or that it is caused to arise in those around the yogi and be directed at him. I knew a woman who was very adept at this. This form of samyama is beneficial and not harmful to the yogi on any level.

25. [By performing samyama] on the strengths [of animals] the strength of an elephant, etc.

This is an element of oriental martial arts and of the magical lore of "primitive" peoples.

26. Knowledge of the small, the hidden or the distant by directing the light of superphysical faculty.

Another yogi whom I knew well told me that when he was three or four years old his mother told him that anything a person might think about was happening somewhere in the world at that very time. This triggered off awareness of a certain ability he, too, must have cultivated in past lives. He told me that he went into the bedroom and sat there fixing his mind on various places in the world in turn and could feel their vibration vividly. Later as an adult he visited those places and found that he had perceived their atmosphere exactly as they truly were. Apparently he discovered the principle of this sutra: If the higher mind is directed to any object, knowledge of that object will be gained.

27. Knowledge of the Solar system by performing Samyama of the Sun.

28. [By performing samyama] on the moon knowledge concerning the arrangement of stars.

29. [By performing samyama] on the pole-star knowledge of their movements.

These three sutras are extremely superficial. Much, much more is obtained by these samyamas, including knowledge of higher and lower worlds, the characteristics of those evolving therein, and the laws governing the coming and goings of the souls in all the worlds. And that is just a fragment of knowledge to be gained.

Therefore it is good to leave all these alone, for we can become captivated by the vast patterns of life perceived and become obsessed like many scientists and philosophers with knowledge simply for its own self.

And so, like one gazing into a crystal or mirror, we can become addicted to such exploration and neglect our life altogether. I have seen many who became utterly consumed by the pursuit of psychic perceptions to the point of becoming unable to live sensibly. A friend of mine told me about a woman he knew who would let her cooking burn because she got so busy talking to La Esmeralda Queen of the Fairies. She eventually became incompetent altogether. This is why the Bhagavad Gita especially emphasizes the practical side of the yoga life.

30. [By performing samyama] on the navel [nabhi] centre [chakra] knowledge of the organization of the body.

The first question here is whether the samyama is to be done on the spinal center opposite the navel or whether it is to be done on the navel itself. It is my observation that concentration in the spine only reveals the causal blueprint of the body in general, but that concentration on the navel reveals the physical body in all its specific details. This has no spiritual application, but gives us an idea how the ancients in India and China had such detailed knowledge of anatomy without practicing dissection on dead bodies. If a person could extend samyama onto the body of another he would then have perfect knowledge of that person's physical constitution.

31. [By performing samyama] on the gullet [kanthakupe–"throat-well"] the cessation of hunger [kshut] and thirst [pipasa].

The center indicated here is the vishuddha chakra at the hollow of the throat. Here, too, the concentration must be on the front of the body to effect the described result. There is no denying that this could have a very practical use, the question being whether such concentration at the time of hunger or thirst would work like the way I have heard people walking down the road in the Indian winter chanting the fire bija ("rung") aloud to alleviate the cold, or whether some degree of siddhi in this concentration for a prolonged time would render it effective. (By the way, I never found that the fire bija made me feel actually warm, but it definitely enabled me to not mind the cold.)

32. [By performing samyama] on the kurma-nadi steadiness [sthairyam].

The kurma nadi is said to be beneath the throat chakra on the front of the body, but it is my speculation that the thymus gland between the heart and throat chakras is the actual point of concentration. The "steadiness" indicated is the state of absolute immobility and immovability of the body. That is, the body becomes incapable of moving or of being moved. This condition has been observed in some yogis in samadhi. Saint Teresa of Avila very often manifested this state when she was not levitating instead. This condition is often listed as intense heaviness.

33. [By performing samyama] the light [jyoti] under the crown of the head [murdha] vision [darshana] of perfected Beings [siddhas].

The word *murdha* simply means head, but translators render it in various ways, according to their experience or lack of it. The thing they nearly all seem to miss is that whether we think it means light within the head, at the back of the head, or above the head, it is all the light of the sahasrara chakra, the thousand-petalled lotus of the astral/causal brain. So if samyama is done on that light the yogi will be able to see the great siddhas, either by their coming to him on their own or through his requesting them for darshan.

There are seven worlds (lokas) or divisions within the manifested creation, and these seven worlds correspond to the seven chakras. Whichever chakra is most active during the individual's lifetime, that will become the "gate" through which he will depart at the time of death and go to that particular region for a while. The sahasrara chakra, the thousand-petalled lotus of the astral and causal brains, corresponds to Satya Loka, which itself is divided into three levels: the lower region of those whose liberation is assured and who are engaging in tapasya for that purpose; those who have advanced enough to be in the middle region where they can already experience the subtle savor of liberation and are being strongly impelled upward; and the higher region of those who are totally liberated but are retaining their capacity to manifest in the regions below in order to assist others in the attainment of liberation. These are the avatars, the "sons of God" who function as saviors in whatever world they enter. This being so, it is likely that it is the light of the upper level of the sahasrara of which Patanjali is speaking, as Taimni indicates by "light under the crown of the head."

34. [Knowledge of] everything [sarvam] from intuition [pratibha].

Pratibha is defined by *A Brief Sanskrit Glossary* as: "Special mental power; imaginative insight; intelligence; splendor of knowledge; intuition; ever-creative activity or consciousness; the spontaneous supreme 'I'-consciousness; Parashakti." That covers a great deal of territory, but we can feel confident that Taimni's translation is the best if we understand intuition as including the insight of direct experience, for that is what samyama is all about fundamentally.

This sutra would appear to be a simple statement that intuition reveals everything, but we should understand that samyama on intuition as an object is implied, and that is a vastly different matter. Plenty of psychics think they are potentially omniscient, but only the yogi really is so through perfection in samyama on pratibha. This is not an overnight or instant occurrence, be assured.

35. [By performing samyama] on the heart [hridaya], awareness [samvit] of the nature of the mind [chitta].

Since previous sutras have been dealing with chakras, we may assume that this one does as well. Nevertheless we must not forget that many yogis consider "heart" to refer to the very core of our being, the Self. Paramhansa Nityananda declared that all the chakras, including the hridaya, were really located in the head, the centers in the trunk of the body, including the chakras in the spine, being only reflections of them.

However that may be, samyama on the hridaya will bring about the samvit, knowledge or awareness, of the chitta, which is not just the energy configuration we call the mind, but the very substance of the mind as well as all the aspects of the mind. In its highest sense, chitta is consciousness itself.

36. Experience [bhoga] is the result of inability to distinguish [avishesha] between the purusha and the sattwa though they are absolutely distinct. Knowledge of the purusha results from samyama on the self-interest [swartha–of the purusha] apart from another's interest [pararthat–of prakriti].

This is an interesting pause in the laundry-listing of how various powers are attained, for this verse deals with experience itself which always binds and blinds the experiencer who cannot distinguish between his true Self and that which the Self is appearing to undergo in the realm of samsara. To become freed from this misperception is to know the Self as it is and thus to be free. So even though samyama is discussed here, the result is really not *a* siddhi but *the* siddhi which brings liberation. So it is an island of atmajnana in the stream of power-seeking.

Here are some other translations of this sutra that may assist in understanding it.

Pandit Usharbudh Arya: "When there is (a conception of) non-distinction between the mental personality and the Conscious Principle, (which are, in fact) totally distinct (and not at commingling, that is called) experience. Through concentration on what is the object of the other (the mental personality) and, separate from that, what is the awareness of the Conscious Principle itself, there arises the realisation of the Conscious Principle."

Vyaas Houston: "Experience is a pratyaya which does not distinguish sattwa (guna of brightness, a primary constituent of matter) and purusha–the self as absolutely unmixed. By samyama on what exists for its own sake (purusha) distinct frpom that (sattwa) which exists for the other–the knowledge of purusha."

Jnaneshwara Bharati: "That having of experiences comes from a presented idea only when there is a commingling of the subtlest aspect of mind (sattwa) and pure consciousness (purusha), which are really quite different. Samyama on the pure consciousness, which is distinct from the subtlest aspect of mind, reveals knowledge of that pure consciousness."

Swami Prabhavananda: "The power of enjoyment arises from a failure to discriminate between the Atman and the sattwa guna, which are totally different. The sattwa guna is merely an agent of the Atman, which is independent, existing only for its own sake. By making samyama on the independence of the Atman, one gains knowledge of the Atman."

Swami Vivekananda: "Enjoyment comes through the non-discrimination of the Soul and sattwa (buddhi) which are totally different. This enjoyment is for the sake of the Soul. There is another state of the sattwa, called svartha (its own pure state). The practice of samyama on this state gives the knowledge of the Purusha."

Before commenting briefly on this sutra myself I wish to recommend that you obtain Tamini's masterly commentary on the Shiva Sutras, *The Ultimate Reality and Realization*. Other commentaries do not even approach the quality of Taimni's insight and ability to communicate such profound wisdom. (That is because he was a proficient yogi.) The Shiva Sutras are a study in how perception of the external vibratory world of prakriti/shakti is possible to a purusha that is nothing but pure consciousness (chaitanya). This understanding is fundamental to anyone wanting to understand the philosophical side of Sanatana Dharma and is even more vital to the yogi who seeks liberation from the net of Maya and naturally needs to know how Maya has arisen and engulfed his experience, binding him to the process of samsara that should be impossible to the purusha. (To be satisfied with the platitudinous statement that both bondage and liberation are illusions is to prove oneself a fool without real interest in knowing Reality.) This book is one of the greatest sources of insight the yogi can possess.

Sattwa in this sutra does not mean the guna as in the Bhagavad Gita, but the subtlest mode of energy (shakti) which is so subtle, so refined, that it is almost non-existent, being the supreme aspect of intelligence (buddhi) that by its near-spirit nature can be perceived by the purusha-spirit, and becomes indistinguishable from consciousness even though it is only an object of consciousness. Again, the Shiva Sutras are necessary to comprehend how this contradiction can exist in our present mode of reality.

Since we do not distinguish between our actual purusha-Self and this sattwa, we experience and identify with the experience, being defined by it. This is being caught in the web of Maya. The web can be cut through by samyama on the true welfare (artha) of the Self (swa). And what does that mean? It means concentration on "Self-ness" and nothing else, concentration on the transcendent nature of the Self. Patanjali is not speaking of "freeing" ideas about the Self, but deep immersion in awareness of the Self as it is: unconditioned and unconditionable, and therefore untouched by experience (bhoga). Obviously this is possible only through perfection in yoga.

37. Thence are produced [jayante] intuitional [pratibha] hearing [shravana], touch [vedan], sight [adarsha], taste [aswada] and smell [varta].

Jnaneshwara Bharati: "From the light of the higher knowledge of that pure consciousness or purusha (3:36) arises higher, transcendental, or divine hearing, touch, vision, taste, and smell." The words used for the five sense faculties/experiences listed here are the same that are used for physical sensory experience, but the qualifying word is *pratibha*, which *A Brief Sanskrit Glossary* defines as "intuition," as does Taimni.

This sutra should usually be taken as referring to the subtle senses of the sukshma sharira, the astral body (actually several layers of astral energy, so really there are several astral bodies, in each of which the five subtle senses are operative). So the yogi is seeing the astral phenomena rather than the physical. It is not long before even the beginning yogi gets some experience of these higher senses.

The yogi can experience every astral object with all five of these senses, something that is impossible on the material plane. So different yogis will experience the same vibration in differing ways according to their inner constitution. For example, many yogis see a bright white light to some extent around holy people, especially around their heads, but others actually smell a heavenly perfume instead, and some hear a subtle sound or heavenly harmony, while other feel the presence of holiness with the subtle sense of touch. One great saint I met many years ago radiated a blazing white fire which I could both see and feel. If I just thought of another saint I would smell perfume utterly different from the fragrances of earth. One time I was speaking with a friend of mine about a monk we both knew who had left his body a year or so before. The moment we began speaking of him the automobile was flooded with the smell of extraordinary incense. A couple of hours later as we drove back from a visit with a yogi we knew, the moment one of us mentioned our departed friend, again the car was filled with the same wonderful scent. Saint Catherine of Sienna could always smell a person's spiritual vibration.

38. They are obstacles [upasargah] in the way of samadhi and powers [siddhayah] when the mind is outward-turned [vytthane].

Jnaneshwara Bharati: "These experiences resulting from samyama are obstacles to samadhi, but appear to be attainments or powers to the outgoing or worldly mind."

In this instance siddhi means attainment of spiritual consciousness resulting from correct yoga practices. Since we all find the physical senses a distraction, it is no surprise that the psychic senses are the same. So although it is necessary that they should develop in us, we must keep the right perspective and not start exploiting them the way materialistic people exploit the physical senses. There really is nothing that cannot be an obstacle to spiritual realization when it is present at the wrong time or in the wrong degree. Since transcendental experience is our prime object, anything other than consciousness itself can be a hindrance. Like a skillful animal trainer we must know how to control and then banish them from our awareness.

39. The mind [chittasya] can enter [avesha] another's body [sharira] on relaxation of the cause [karana] of bondage [bandha] and from knowledge of passages [prachara].

Pandit Usharbudh Arya: "By loosening the cause of bondage and learning the (paths of) circulation (of mental energy) (the yogi learns to) enter and take possession of another body."

Jnaneshwara Bharati: "By loosening or letting go of the causes of bondage and attachment, and by following the knowledge of how to go forth into the passages of the mind, there comes the ability to enter into another body."

Swami Prabhavananda: "When the bonds of the mind caused by karma have been loosened, the yogi can enter into the body of another by knowledge of the operation of its nerve currents."

Swami Vivekananda: "When the cause of bondage has become loosened, the yogi, by his knowledge of its channels of activity of the chitta, enters another body."

There are two ways of "entering" another's body. One is a literal entering into someone's body and controlling it, living through it just as though it were one's own. This is said to have been done by Shankaracharya and other yogis on rare occasions. Discarnate beings are able to do the same through their astral awareness, as in possession and mediumship.

Rajasi Janakananda told that when he had an extremely dangerous brain operation he left his body immediately upon being anesthetized and went into higher worlds. When he returned to his body, from afar he saw that Yogananda was in his body. The Master smiled and waved at him, and suddenly he was back in his body. Rajasi said that Yogananda had entered his body and kept it from dying on the operating table.

The other way a person "enters" someone's body is through a kind of mental projection rather than a complete entry with the subtle body. The person is able to literally move around through the body and observe it intimately. Some healers do this for diagnosis and healing.

The only doctor I have ever trusted totally was the great Dr. Josef Lenninger, who was given asylum in America to evade the many attempts of Hitler to force him back to Germany because of his renown in that country in relation to his vast medical knowledge. After the First World War the German government sent Dr. Lenninger around the world studying indigenous medicine. He spent the most time in South India with a sadhu, Rishi Krishnananda, who was a great practitioner of Ayurveda. From him Dr. Lenninger learned to develop this siddhi by means of which he could send his mind into another's body and know all about it. For example, he could tell anyone their blood pressure, body temperature, condition of all their organs, any surgeries they had undergone, what major illnesses they had had since birth, and even their birthday! He could also tell anyone the exact state of health of their mother and father. Once I showed him a photo of a great yogi who had left his body a few months before. Dr. Lenninger told me exactly the condition of his health for many previous years and even described his death and its causes. On occasion he would draw an illness or problematical condition from the patient's body into his own and cure it there, sometimes immediately and sometimes with treatment over some time.

I knew a yogi in Western India who continually healed people in this way. The first time I met him he was curing himself of diabetes that he had taken on himself two or three weeks before. Such an ability is extremely risky and its wisdom can certainly be questioned.

40. By mastery over udana, levitation and non-contact with water, mire, thorns etc.

Jnaneshwara Bharati: "By the mastery over udana, the upward flowing prana vayu, there is a cessation of contact with mud, water, thorns, and other such objects, and there ensues the rising or levitation of the body."

This is how yogis walk on water or do not sink in quicksand or mud. They also can walk over broken glass or other sharp points and not be pierced. They do this by means of levitation, either by rising some distance above those things or inducing a mild form of this siddhi wherein they touch the objects physically but are weightless and so come to no harm.

41. By mastery over samana, blazing of gastric fire.

Jnaneshwara Bharati: "By mastery over samana, the prana flowing in the navel area, there comes effulgence, radiance, or fire."

Yogis often shine with light, sometimes with the very practical aim of lighting up a dark place. Taimni is the only translator I know of that considers the siddhi to manifest as powerful gastric power of digestion, but since samana governs digestion it is not without possibility. Certainly this siddhi has been used by yogis to subsist on food impossible for normal people to digest, and has also been employed to destroy any poison they may have ingested. On more than one occasion Maharshi Dayananda Saraswati was poisoned by those who hated his teaching on the necessity to reform Hinduism, but was able to survive through this siddhi. Srimati Maitri Devi, a saint living in New Delhi, told me that her guru employed this siddhi when the pandits of Benares poisoned her, jealous of her superior knowledge of the shastras and daring to be a woman, to boot!

42. By performing samyama on the relation between akasha and the ear [shrotra]: superphysical [divyam: celestial; divine] hearing.

Each of the five elements corresponds to one of the five senses. Earth, water, fire, and air correspond to smell, taste, sight, and touch respectively. These four are totally passive. But the sense that arises from ether (akasha) is both passive and active: the power of speech and the faculty of hearing that speech. It is the power known as Vak, which means both Speech and Word. Yet it also includes hearing. This is why sound is such a powerful force in spiritual development and therefore in the technique of yoga, especially the subtle, mental sound of thought. We can change our very nature (prakriti) by both projecting and hearing mantric sounds. This is a cornerstone of sadhana. The yoga adept becomes extremely sensitive to the effects of all kinds of sounds, and knows how to use this sensitivity to determine that which is most conducive to mental calm and stability. Classical Indian music, instrumental and vocal, is based on yogic perception.

Samyama on the faculty of hearing and the subtle akasha awaken the faculty of the spiritual ear. This is not to be confused with either astral or causal "hearing" or clairaudience. Rather, it is best described as being a kind of intuition-experience of hearing. But nothing really conveys its full nature but the experience itself.

43. By performing Samyama on the relation between the body and akasha and at the same time bringing about coalescence of the mind with light [things like] cotton down [there comes the power of] passage through space.

This is a very interesting sutra. In treatises on yoga and meditation the faculty of the mental energies to take the form of whatever is being looked at or concentrated on is frequently mentioned as the basis for certain yogic practices. Here Patanjali tells us that a steady and purely one-pointed awareness of light objects stimulates the faculty of levitation and movement through space. This is not just theory. My friend Durga Prasad Sahai, a disciple of Swami Keshabananda who is written about in *Autobiography of a Yogi*, told me that he was very well acquainted with Ganga Baba, a saint who lived at the source of the Ganges (Gangotri). Ganga Baba could often be seen flying through the air. When the border conflict was going on between India and China, all travel into Tibet was absolutely forbidden. But Ganga Baba asked the government officers to issue him a permit to visit Lhasa. Not wanting to refuse the saint, they just delayed and delayed. Finally, after six months, permission was granted. When Ganga Baba went to their offices and expressed his thanks for the permit, they prostrated before him and begged: "Forgive us, Baba, our agents in Lhasa say they see you there nearly every day, even though you are returning here each night." Ganga Baba was not bilocating–going from one place to another in a moment, which also is a yoga power–but was really flying to Tibet whenever he wanted to. So he told Durga Prasad.

The opposite is also possible: a yogi can make himself so heavy he is immovable and nothing can pick him up or carry him. In the early days of Western contact with the Hawaiian islands it was noticed that the Hawaiian divers could sink much faster to the ocean floor than anyone else and could also stay underwater for a longer time. When they were asked their secret they told them that kahunas had taught them to feel that they were rocks when they dropped into the water. And it worked. As Sri Ramakrishna often said: "The mind is everything."

44. The power of contacting the state of consciousness which is outside the intellect and is therefore inconceivable is called mahavideha. From it is destroyed the covering of light.

Videha means "bodiless," and Mahavideha is the Great Disembodiment of consciousness.

Obviously the consciousness of the embodied yogi is confined, whereas the consciousness of the disembodied yogi is without boundaries, limitless and free. Yet, the limitless, disembodied Reality is within the body as well. Therefore it is not a matter of projecting the consciousness outside the body or "astral traveling," but of going even deeper within to the core point, the true heart (hridaya) where the body has no influence at all, but Infinity abides undimmed and unconfined.

"Outside the intellect" (or mind) does not mean outside the body. This is very important, since a great deal of yogis think that some kind of outer projection is needed, and some schools of thought consider that unless a person leaves the body and passes through higher worlds there is no spiritual progress, much less liberation. This is the direct opposite of the way things really are. It means to be withdrawn from the intellect, the jnanamaya kosha, and the will, the anandamaya kosha, and becoming bodiless in consciousness even though still in the body. Only yogis can understand this, much less accomplish it.

In the prior section, in sutra 52, we were told that the fourth pranayama also dissolves the covering of the atmic light. So if this seems too abstract or difficult, we can still resort to pranayama for the same result.

45. Mastery over the pancha-bhutas by performing samyama on their gross, constant, subtle, all-pervading and functional states.

This applies to each of the Great Elements. The yogi may choose which ones he wishes to master, or of course work with all of them. Only a person adept in meditation could even begin to do this, because the "gross, constant, subtle, all-pervading and functional states" cannot be learned from books, but must be the personal experience of the yogi. This not gained in a day, and perhaps not even in a single lifetime.

46. Thence, the attainment of animan etc., perfection of the body and the non-obstruction of its functions [of the body] by the powers [of the elements].

The body of such a yogi then becomes a mirror of his momentary bhava or the focus of his will. For example, I once saw a photograph of Anandamayi Ma looking at an image of Shiva she was holding in her hand. Her face was an identical duplicate of the face of Shiva. Her appearance was constantly changing, so that no photograph really "looked" like her. Only motion pictures could convey what she looked like. I had literally seen about two hundred photographs of her before I met her, yet when I saw her I did not recognize her at all. I only knew it was her because I had seen her two attendants in several photographs with her, and they looked just like their photos. I have seen Ma be the tallest person in a room (except for me) and within twenty minutes be the shortest one there. One moment she would looked aged and the next appear young.

47. Beauty, fine complexion, strength and adamantine hardness constitute the perfection of the body.

These qualities are really the perfections of the mind, the body only following after it. The word *bala*, here translated "strength," also means "young" or "youthful," just as I described regarding the appearance of Ma Anandamayi. I witnessed these qualities in more than one adept yogi, but thoroughly in Swami Sivananda of Rishikesh.

48. Mastery over the sense-organs by performing samyama on their power of cognition, real nature, egoism [asmita], all-pervasiveness and functions.

Asmita is really better defined in *A Brief Sanskrit Glossary*: I-ness; the sense of "I am;" "I exist;" sense of individuality. It is the senses (indriyas) that give us this sense of asmita.

49. Thence, instantaneous cognition without the use of any vehicle and complete mastery over pradhana.

Pradhana is prakriti: causal matter. Therefore a yogi can alter anything by his mere thought, just as Jesus turned water into wine and Sri Gajanana Maharaj of Nasik could turn wine into milk and mutton into roses.

50. Only from the awareness of the distinction between sattwa and purusha arise supremacy over all states and forms of existence [omnipotence] and knowledge of every thing [omniscience].

Perception of the distinction between sattwa and the atman (purusha) is almost impossible because it is extremely subtle, and very, very few yogis' intellects (buddhi) are so subtle as to reveal it, and even fewer yogis have the intelligence to recognize it. This is part of the final step to liberation (moksha).

First we must understand as well as we can the nature of sattwa. To do that we must turn to the supreme scripture of yoga (yoga shastra), the Bhagavad Gita. A thorough knowledge of the Gita is essential for the yogi, for without the instruction given there it is virtually impossible to attain the supreme realization. If people were grounded in the teachings of the Gita they would never go astray or be fooled by either their own minds or by unscrupulous "gurus" and "authorities" whose fundamental error and unworthiness would be revealed to them by the clear and simple truths found there. A yogi and his thoughts should be inseparable from the Gita, which has no equal in all the world. Those who do not base themselves on the Gita will fail and fall in time. This I have seen over and over.

So then, what does the Gita tells us about sattwa?

"Sattwa is stainless, luminous, and health-giving; it binds by attachment to happiness and by attachment to knowledge" (Bhagavad Gita 14:6). Although the human mind in its ordinary condition cannot even conceive of the Self fully, yet the yogi through the agency of his totally purified intellect (buddhi) can do so through the medium of sattwa guna. It is well known to the yogis that sattwa is so subtle it is almost always indistinguishable from the atman. Yet it reveals the atman to the adept yogi. The usual function of sattwa guna is to impel the individual to seek the bliss of the Self and the knowledge required to know the Self. When that is fulfilled perfectly, then sattwa reveals the Self.

Yet, as the Gita says, sattwa is not the Self and therefore like any external, material force or object, can influence and even bind us. Three verses later, the Gita tell us: "Sattwa causes attachment to happiness" (Bhagavad Gita 14:9). That is, those who are not yogis relentlessly intent on the Self can become addicted to mere happiness and, contented with that, no longer fervently seek the revelation of the Self. Sattwa cannot render us blind to the Self, but it can distract us from the Self. Although sattwa illumines the intellect, it also functions on a lower level. It is extremely subtle and extremely pure, yet it is feeling-based, separate from both mind (manas) and intellect (buddhi). As a consequence it is possible for it to be a hindrance and distraction.

When it is not detrimental through the weakness of the resolve and understanding of the individual yogi, sattwa is a supreme blessing. So the Gita tells us: "When the light of knowledge shines in all the gates of the body, then it should be known that sattwa is dominant" (14:11). "When the embodied one dies when sattwa is dominant, then he enters the stainless realms of the knowers of the Highest" (14:14). "From sattwa arises knowledge" (14:17). "Those established in sattwa go upward [to higher realms]" (14:18).

After revealing the Self, sattwa remains. "That happiness... born of the light of one's own Self, is declared to be sattwic" (Bhagavad Gita 18:37).

Through the development of shuddha-sattwa, supremely pure sattwa, the potentially infinite realm of the Self is opened and entered to dwell in forevermore.

51. By non-attachment even to that, on the very seed of bondage being destroyed, follows kaivalya.

"That" refers to the "supremacy over all states and forms of existence and knowledge of every thing" mentioned in the previous verse. As could be expected, it is extremely difficult to be indifferent and detached from such power and knowledge. Yet the yogi must be, otherwise bondage will not be destroyed and kaivalya, the transcendental state of absolute freedom from conditioned existence that is perfect liberation, will not be attained. Trapped by the glory of aishwarya, the divine power and glory that is the reflection of the immanent God, Ishwara, there is every likelihood of the yogi falling down to further bondage, even to complete loss of the development he had gained through yoga. Even worse, he may come to believe that he is Ishwara himself.

During my first trip to India I met the fore-mentioned disciple of Swami Keshabananda. He told me of amazing things he had witnessed, including Keshvananda's materialization in physical form years after his death. But Yogananda had said that the great yogi had failed to attain liberation in that lifetime because of his attachment to miracles.

If, however, the yogi can be disinterested in the glories of the state described in this and the previous sutra, then "the very seed of bondage" will be destroyed and liberation attained. What, then, is the future of those yogis that are elated over even the simplest of yogic experiences or the opening of elementary psychic abilities? Especially if they tell about them? Not much, we can be assured.

Without supreme vairagya–non-attachment, dispassion, disinterest and even aversion for all conditions and attainments whatsoever–a yogi will not make any significant progress. Like people rowing a boat while the anchor is down, he will get nowhere and will have wasted his life.

52. [There should be] avoidance of pleasure or pride on being invited by the super-physical entities in charge of various planes because there is the possibility of the revival of evil.

This idea of yogis being approached by astral beings and led astray from the path is almost completely ignored at the present time. Actually, I have only heard one yogi speak about this subject and that was over fifty years ago. Nevertheless this is a long-established concept in India and one recorded in many traditional religious texts.

Astral beings may approach a yogi for various motivations. Some among the gods, for example, are said to fear that the yogi will attain to their positions in the higher worlds, so they seek to ruin his sadhana and bring about his fall. Some beings are simply malicious, hating human beings and wishing to harm them in any way possible. Others may simply be foolish and have no idea they are doing anything detrimental. The one yogi I mentioned spoke in detail about the ways astral beings try to deceive humans, saying that they even may use other human beings to attain their goal.

The Buddhists are very aware of this also, but perhaps the Eastern Christians are the most intent on the need to guard against astral deception. All practicers of the mystical tradition known as Hesychia (Silence) are warned about such danger, and many incidents are cited as proof of its reality, many of them from our own time. As a novice in an Eastern Christian monastery I heard a great deal about this, including experiences of people well known to some of the members.

Fear should have no place in the life of a yogi, but wise caution and wariness certainly should be a constant factor for him. Contact with astral beings of any kind, including departed human beings, real or supposed, can only bring harm to the yogi and his yoga. Just as in the human body various parts are isolated so elements harmful to one area do not invade another, so it is in (and within) the various worlds.

Painful as it may be to us, absolute separation from the departed is beneficial to a human being. Interchange with the dead can be truly deadly. The only exception is when spiritually developed people help earthbound spirits to pass on to the astral realms where they can evolve. Otherwise contact of the living with the dead is detrimental to both sides. And there is grave danger of deceitful spirits approaching sincere people and appealing for help when they really want to create a bond between them so they can manipulate the embodied person. Often possession is their intention.

Both the embodied and the disembodied should stay in their proper realms and look to their evolution. A wise principle was stated by Sri Ramakrishna to his disciple Niranjan who was being used as a medium by a group of spiritualists in Calcutta: "My son, think of ghosts and you will become a ghost. Think of God and you will become God. Which to you prefer?"

53. Knowledge born of awareness of Reality by performing samyama on moment and [the process of] its succession.
54. From it (vivekajam-jnanam) knowledge of distinction between similars which cannot be distinguished by class, characteristic or position.

Again it should be pointed out that samyama is extraordinarily difficult, and as rare as it is difficult. This is because it just cannot be taught to anyone in the usual manner. Either you intuit it (with no assurance that your intuition is correct) or you just stumble onto it (with no assurance that what you did was samyama). There is no doubt in my mind that a great master can in some manner transfer the knowledge of samyama directly into the mind of the student, but even that is chancy. I have come across a lot of "transmitted vidya" that was nothing more than imagination, and pretty low level imagination at that. So I would advise that the subject be forgotten about until a competent teacher comes into the orbit of the yogi's life. And there is every likelihood that a competent teacher will not teach samyama to him lest it become an obstacle or a source of delusion.

Anyhow, those who can do samyama on both the moment and the way it "becomes" or "passes on" to the next moment can come to understand the deepest roots of anything and can distinguish easily between things that seem absolutely the same, yet are not. For some things are mere bubbles soon to dissolve and other things are substantial and can be worked with to the advantage of the yogi. The ability to tell the difference is a necessary ability.

It becomes obvious that there are certain very tenuous and unsure aspects of yoga that are best left alone until they are presented in a way that leaves no room for doubt or deception.

55. The highest knowledge born of the awareness of Reality is transcendent, includes the cognition of all objects simultaneously, pertains to all objects and processes whatsoever in the past, present and future and also transcends the world process.

The word Taimni translates as "highest knowledge" is actually *tarakam*: that which enables one to cross over or transcend samsara. Such a knowledge is all pervading; that is, it encompasses all that is/are evolving within the cosmos. Nothing is unknown to it. It is divine omniscience participated in by the liberated spirit. But it is not confined to relative existence. It also encompasses that which is transcendent, beyond all relativity. Incredible as it seems, while remaining finite the liberated person (purusha) enters into a state of consciousness that includes (encompasses) the absolute Parabrahman itself. And this is necessary because Brahman, the Paramatman, is the essential being of the jivatman. The individual spirit (jiva) cannot know itself and not simultaneously know Brahman, because though distinct they are inseparable. It is a mystery, and it is foolish for the human mind to puzzle over it and try to figure it out and even attempt to imagine what it must be like. Rather, each one of us must strive to attain that status. "Therefore be a yogi" (Bhagavad Gita 6:46).

56. Kaivalya is attained when there is equality of purity between the purusha and sattwa.

The following alternate translations can help us in comprehending the meaning of this sutra:

Jnaneshwar: "With the attainment of equality between the purest aspect of sattwic buddhi and the pure consciousness of purusha, there comes absolute liberation, and that is the end."

Prabhavananda: "Perfection is attained when the mind becomes as pure as the Atman itself."

Purohit Swami: "When the intellect become as pure as the Self, liberation follows."

Usually when we encounter the word "sattwa" we think of sattwa guna, the quality of energy (shakti or prakriti) that has the characteristics of light, purity, harmony, and goodness. But because the most purified and refined intellect, the buddhi, is clear light, it has itself come to be referred to as sattwa. All the lower aspects of our makeup eventually drop away or are dissolved, but the sattwic buddhi is said to be absorbed or assumed into the Self so only the Self remains. Sri Ramana Maharshi spoke of this as a fact: "The buddhi becomes the Self."

When, therefore, all else drops away and the buddhi possessing the quality of shuddhi-sattwa, pure light, merges into the Self, "kaivalya is attained." *A Brief Sanskrit Glossary* gives this definition of kaivalya: transcendental state of Absolute Independence; state of absolute freedom from conditioned existence; moksha; isolation; final beatitude; emancipation.

Kaivalya-mukti is liberation.

And that is all that can be said about the inexpressible state.

Kaivalya Pada:
Yoga Sutras Book IV

This is a very interesting yet somewhat puzzling section of the Yoga Sutras because it covers a variety of subjects seemingly at random, though more than one sutra may be devoted to a single subject. However it may be, here it is.

1. The Siddhis are the result of birth, drugs, mantras, austerities or samadhi.

Patanjali listed various siddhis in the Sadhana Pada: Book II. He also outlined which of the yamas or niyamas would lead to those siddhis. We can question as to whether he is harking back to them or is giving us a blanket exposition relating to any other psychic powers that may arise in the sadhaka. I personally think the latter is correct and will approach it from that viewpoint. There are five possible sources or producers of the siddhis.

Birth [janma]. This means that siddhis can be carried over from previous births in which they were developed, that they are a part of the person's samskaras.

Drugs [aushadhi]. At the time of Patanjali allopathic drugs and the various concoctions current today were not known. "Aushadhi" means herb-based. It is well known that certain herbs or plants can produce psychic abilities that usually disappear as the effect of the drug wears off, though there can remain a kind of heightened sensitivity or mental distortion that is at best borderline pathological.

Patanjali is not advocating the use of herbs or plants to develop siddhis. Rather, he is informing us that siddhis are not always signposts of psychic development or spiritual evolution, but merely the result of having ingested certain herbs or plants. Some unfortunate individuals are permanently damaged physically or psychically by these plants and consider themselves enlightened or possessing some exalted status. This, too, is pathological. No real yogi countenances the use of such substances.

Mantra. It is well known in India that certain mantras can bestow powers on those who attain what is known as "mantra siddhi." There are even certain places in India where a person can attain mantra siddhi more rapidly than in an ordinary location.

For decades, a man simply called Poison King cured people of snakebite. The government of India had arranged that to send a telegram to him to report someone needing neutralization of poison, including cobra venom, a person need only use the address "Poison King." The telegram would be rushed to him. He always carried a towel slung over one shoulder, and when he got a telegram he would tear a narrow strip off the towel while reciting a mantra. Instantly the person would be free of the effects of the poison.

I met a man who had the same siddhi. Through mantra he had actually brought back to life a man declared dead by a hospital in New Delhi. Being "scientific" the hospital refused to acknowledge the fact and cancel the death certificate. So the man remained legally dead for the rest of his life!

I have known of people who cured illness through mantra and also were able to know what was going on at a distance and to know the future through mantra. Obviously liberation (moksha) is the best fruit of mantra sadhana.

Tapasya. Spiritual practice, though undertaken for the purpose of enlightenment, can also bestow siddhis on a person, either by producing them or awakening siddhis gained in a previous life. Worthy teachers are therefore always cautioning sadhakas to be very wary of such siddhis and to make sure that they do not distract them from the only worthwhile goal: Self-realization. During my own sadhana I have had various psychic abilities arise that I found absolutely worthless and distracting. Since it is said that you can lose siddhis by talking about them, I would either write to friends or tell them about these abilities and in a short time they would fade away.

Samadhi. There are various forms of samadhi, but all are states of superconsciousness, though some are more conducive to enlightenment than others. Nevertheless, it is natural that superconscious experience should produce siddhis as they are natural characteristics of life in the higher levels or worlds within creation. So those who elevate their consciousness even here in the earth plane may cause their unfoldment since they were already inherent in us when we were just an atom of hydrogen.

2. The transformation from one species or kind into another is by the overflow of natural tendencies or potentialities [prakriti].

Jnaneswara Bharati: "The transition of transformation into another form or type of birth takes place through the filling in of their innate nature."

Prabhavananda: "The transformation of one species into another is cause by the inflowing of nature."

The more science advances in real discoveries, the more Sanatana Dharma is revealed as the mathematics of both the material and spiritual realms. Unfortunately people do not come to the realization that it is dharma that validates science, not the other way around. If this was realized, serious search and research in the texts of ancient India would be commonplace.

Shortly after returning from my first trip to India I met a man who loaned me some recordings of talks by one of the major figures in physics in America. This man had gone to India and traveled some years in the south searching out palm leaf manuscripts on scientific subjects. He managed quite well, and when he returned to America he went to one of the most prestigious universities where he was to teach that year and talked about his discoveries. The heads of the physics department were jubilant and declared that as soon as possible they would arrange an international gathering of physicists at which he could present his finding. "You will completely revolutionize the entire field of physics," they told him, "and your name will head the list of those whose research brought about major breakthroughs in science." "But these are not my discoveries!" he protested. "I learned everything I have told you about by studying ancient manuscripts in south India. The credit goes to those who wrote them, not me." "Oh, well, in that case we won't be bothering with it," they told him. He was so disgusted he resigned his professorship and began teaching metaphysics integrated with physics, which really is just what the Sankhya and Yoga philosophies are today.

In the nineteenth century when Darwin's theories were turning the world upside down for religionists and scientists in the West, the yogis of India could not understand the fuss. The yogic sages had known about evolution in its full meaning for thousands of years. And this simple verse explains why and how evolution occurs. The individual spirit (jiva) enters a form in relative creation and lives and functions through the form until it has learned to perfectly manifest all the potentials of that form. When it has done so, it passes on into the next more complex form and "fills in" that. And so it goes until the jiva has traversed the entire range of evolution and developed the capacity to share in the infinity of God the Absolute and entered into total, perfect and eternal union with God.

As Shakespeare wrote, "all the world's a stage" with the individual spirits wearing their costumes and playing their parts. Just as actors begin with small parts and progress to bigger roles by demonstrating their skill in those smaller parts, so also do the spirits advance to higher and more complex forms of existence and consciousness through taking on and perfecting their identity and functions within the evolutionary forms of creation, at last returning home to God.

Because of the incalculable length of time this process of return requires, God breathes forth the creation many times in cycles. Creation, being an activity of the eternal God, is also eternal. It never began, and will never end. Instead, it runs in alternating cycles of manifestation-projection and withdrawal. Nothing is destroyed, simply recycled.

The first "character" in the cosmic drama as it unfolds is a single atom of hydrogen. This is the first body, the first "role" in which the newly-projected spirit finds itself. Then in its implanted will, tending back to the divine, it builds more and more complex atomic and molecular structures in the struggle to manifest full self-awareness. This entails an almost infinitely long series of progressively more complex and evolved body vehicles, each of which the spirit must both project around itself and function in to attain and manifest the fullest consciousness possible in those vehicles. Oliver Wendel Holmes, one of many great Americans whose belief in reincarnation is conveniently overlooked, wrote in his poem, "The Chambered Nautilus:"

> Build thee more stately mansions, O my soul!
> As the swift seasons roll!
> Leave thy low-vaulted past!
> Let each new temple, nobler than the last,
> Shut thee from heaven with a dome more vast,
> Till thou at length art free,
> Leaving thine outgrown shell by life's unresting sea!

The drama of creation, simply stated, is this: God breathes forth this vast universe. Slowly it comes out and evolves according to set patterns. Then after a precise measure of time, he breathes it back in again, involves it, and it vanishes. This he does eternally. Mostly the same actors are in the successive dramas, though they evolve to bigger and (hopefully) better roles.

God breathes forth himself as creation, and the individual spirit comes down and is first of all embodied in an atom of hydrogen. As time passes, it builds more and more complex atomic and molecular structures. From gas to mineral to plant to animal, so develops the career of the individual spirit's drama of evolution. As the Sufi poet, Rumi, wrote:

> A stone I died and rose again a plant.
> A plant I died and rose an animal;
> I died an animal and was born a man.
> Why should I fear? What have I lost by death?
> As man, death sweeps me from this world of men
> That I may wear an angel's wings in heaven;
> Yet e'en as angel may I not abide,
> For nought abideth save the face of God.
> Thus o'er the angels' world I wing my way
> Onwards and upwards, unto boundless lights;
> Then let me be as nought, for in my heart
> Rings as a harp-song that we must return to Him.

At all stages along the way, we find organisms in which the differing levels overlap. In the sea we find entities which are simultaneously plant and animal, and on land we have those that have developed an elementary sense of touch and locomotion, such as the Venus flytrap. In human form there are those who are to some degree still animal. In the intervals between embodiments, the spirit spends time in the astral and causal regions where awakening and growth also take place. (This is best explained in the forty-third chapter of *Autobiography of a Yogi* by Paramhansa Yogananda.)

3. The incidental cause does not move or stir up the natural tendencies into activity; it merely removes the obstacles, like a farmer [irrigating a field].

"One acts according to one's own prakriti–even the wise man does so. Beings follow their own prakriti" (Bhagavad Gita 3:33). Prakriti is everything: the vibrating energy from which all forms and impulses of various sorts are produced. Prakriti in this instance includes the eternal impulse to evolve to enlightenment. Nothing produces this impulse; it is inherent in the energy-being (prakriti) of each one of us. It is this impulse that has impelled us from life to life, evolving from most simple to most complex, from unconsciousness to self-consciousness. It is not an external force, but the inmost movement arising directly from the Self (atman). Therefore Patanjali says that nothing in relative experience produces or stimulates evolution and ultimate enlightenment. Rather, the eternal part of us is moving us along that evolutionary path. This being so, the various spiritual practices we call sadhana or tapasya do not and absolutely cannot lead to liberation. Yoga removes the obstacles to realization, and then it does not even occur, it is revealed as being already present.

A farmer digs a trench up to a stream, then removes the last bit of earth between it and the stream and the water flows into the field. The water has always been there, but the earth was blocking its flow. The pressure of the water impelled it into the field, not the earth nor the farmer. The water is our prakriti, the farmer is ourself, and the earth is the obstacles removed by our practice of yoga.

Before leaving this sutra, it should be pointed out that there is a misunderstanding based on the truth that no external agent can bring about our spiritual development and moksha. The mistake is the conclusion that nothing need be done for our liberation, that to do anything will compound our delusion and prevent our enlightenment. Often this results in its adherents doing absolutely nothing but accepting their status as already enlightened beings. Others engage in a variety of "doing nothing" methods. Both kinds talk a great deal as do the Protestant Fundamentalists who "live by faith" and "take on faith" their salvation. Simply believing and proclaiming is their salvation. And it makes their "advaita teachers" a great deal of money.

But the sutra gives us a very important fact: *there are actions that remove the obstacles to enlightenment.* Therefore methodology in the form of yogic processes or kriyas are not only legitimate, without them the reality of the Self will not be authentically perceived or manifested. Liberation may be claimed, but it will not be anything more than words. As the Gita tells us: "Be a yogi" (6:46).

4. Artificially created minds [proceed] from egoism [asmita] alone.

Jnaneshwara Bharati: "The emergent mind fields spring forth from the individuality of I-ness (asmita)."

Shearer: "All minds are created by Ego–the separative sense of 'I.'"

Born into relative existence with the feeling of separate, individual existence (asmita), a mind develops along with the other bodies that have been taken on by the Self. As they are in a sense artificial, not native to, or inherent in, the Self, so also is the mind that is created by asmita.

Such a mind is ever-changing and is at best a kind of phantom. Those who base their action on such a mind are themselves like shifting sands without continuity and often ignorantly think that they have no abiding self but are themselves a perpetually changing phantom.

Patanjali wants us to understand the fundamental unreliability of such a mind because it is basically non-existent since it will die the death of the body. Only that which is forever existent is real. Those things that come into existence and go out of existence are but dreams; as I say: phantoms. "It is known that the unreal never comes to be, and the real never ceases to be" (Bhagavad Gita 2:16).

The yogi, therefore, does not bother much with the ego-created mind, but ignores it and applies himself to sadhana which will drastically alter that mind and eventually dissolve it so consciousness will prevail rather than any form of mind. Yogis do not "work" with the asmita-based mind, but engage in yoga that reveals the true Self which needs no such kind of a mind. Such a mind is a ghost, and those who struggle with it and try to change it are truly fighting the air. Such activity has its compensation, though, because it strengthens and establishes identity with the ego. So the ignorant love to mind-game and speak of "getting rid of the ego."

5. The one [natural] mind is the director or mover of the many [artificial] minds in their different activities.

Jnaneshwara Bharati: "While the activities of the emergent mind fields may be diverse, the one mind is the director of the many."

Vivekananda: "Though the activities of the different created minds are various, the one original mind is the controller of them all."

Here we need a very broad concept of "mind." Actually the original mind is really our original consciousness and is not at all what the created, asmita-based minds are. It may temporarily control or direct those minds, but it also is what dissolves them ultimately.

What Patanjali wants us to understand is that the real part of us is always in control of the unreal part, however unaware of that fact we may be. Everything, even illusion, depends upon reality. Just as driftwood floats on the surface of the ocean and is moved by it up and down, hither and thither, yet the driftwood is in no way the ocean or the ocean the driftwood. In the same way the Self is completely in charge of the non-self (not-self), yet is not the non-self any more than the non-self can ever be the Self.

This may seem like word juggling or empty philosophizing, but it has a very practical purpose: the realization that nothing exists or moves independently of either the Supreme Self (Paramatman) or the individual Self (jivatman). Just as the dreamer is the only reality, and not the dream, so the Self is the sole reality in change of the illusory bodies that appear to be part of our being, but in actuality have nothing at all to do with us. Only through yoga is this seen and acted upon.

6. Of these the mind born of meditation is free from impressions [samskaras].

Jnaneshwara Bharati: "Of these mind fields, the one that is born from meditation is free from any latent impressions that could produce karma."

"The mind born of meditation" is not really a mind like the others, as I have said, but is consciousness, the light of the Self. By "impressions" is meant karmas or samskaras. Since the Self cannot be affected by karma or samskara, the consciousness that dawns through meditation is utterly free of them. Only those who live through and in this meditation-born mind can be free of karma and samskara. Yogis do not "work out" or "reap" karma, they step back from it, transcend it and become untouched (and untouchable) by it. In the same way they become free from any form of samskara. Those who abide in the Self have no karma or samskara.

7. Karmas are neither white nor black [neither good nor bad] in the case of yogis, they are of three kinds in the case of others.

Vivekananda: "Works [karmas] are neither black nor white for the yogis; for others they are threefold [black, white and mixed]."

The word "yogis" does not mean merely anyone who engages in yoga practice, but an adept yogi, one, according to Vyas Houston, who is living in the state of yoga described in the second verse of the Yoga Sutras as: *chitta-vritti-nirodhah*–the inhibition [nirodhah] of the modifications [vritti] of the mind [chitta]. When no action can produce a reaction or wave in the mind of the yogi, then he is in the state of yoga. For such a one actions are neither positive (white) or negative (black), nor do they result in positive or negative effects. They result in no effects on either the mind or the external life circumstances of the yogi. "He acts untainted by evil as a lotus leaf is not wetted by water" (Bhagavad Gita 5:10).

For others, however, all actions produce reactions, either positive or negative or a mixture of both positive and negative effects. For them every action without exception produces karmic reaction.

8. From these only those tendencies [vasanas] are manifested for which the conditions are favorable.

Jnaneshwara Bharati: "Those threefold actions result in latent impressions [vasanas] that will later arise to fruition only corresponding to those impressions."

Swami Prabhavananda: "Of the tendencies [vasanas] produced by these three kinds of karma, only those are manifested for which the conditions are favorable."

There is a Pali verse that says: "I have nothing but my actions, and I shall never have anything but my actions." The samskaras remain in the subtle bodies of the individual and manifest only when the outer conditions are favorable or corresponding to them. If it takes tens of thousand of years for them to manifest, so it shall be. And if the right conditions arise shortly after their impression in the mind, even in the same life they were created, they will manifest. This is why from life to life markedly dissimilar karmas may manifest. For example, one life can be a manifestation of predominately negative karmas and in the next life mostly positive karmas. Personalities are the manifestation of karmas (vasanas), so an individual's personality in one life can be opposite to that of his previous life. That is why in past life recall people find that in one life they are of a spiritual inclination, and in the very next life of a purely material inclination. That is why we must right now seize the opportunity to practice yoga diligently and dissolve the karmic store and end rebirth.

This verse indicates to us that there is an interaction: the karmas determine the life conditions in a birth, and the conditions determine which karmas shall come to fruition. This is an important point, necessary for a complete understanding of karma and karmic force. Karma is not an almighty, irresistible force. That is why the yogi can modify or erase his karmas.

9. There is the relation of cause and effect even though separated by class, locality and time because memory and impressions are the same in form.

Jnaneshwara Bharati: "Since memory (smriti) and the deep habit patterns (samskaras) are the same in appearance, there is an unbroken continuity in the playing out of those traits, even though there might be a gap in location, time, or state of life."

Just as there are no hitches or glitches in the flow of time, but there is a unity of movement in its unfoldment, in the same way because memory and samskaras are fundamentally identical in nature the individual experiences an unbroken flow of cause and effect in his life, so much so that the awareness or impulse of the arising of the samskara and the samskara itself seem to be the same thing. Therefore "a gap in location, time, or state of life" is not evident, though actual.

Consequently a person is usually not aware that an impulse from within may have been resting and incubating there for many past lives. This is one of the reasons people do not realize they have lived before. Nearly everyone asks, as did I: "If I have lived before, why don't I remember it?" when in actuality almost every impulse or reaction we have is itself a memory from a past life, but so perfectly "present" that we do not realize it. The stream of our present life is really our past lives flowing on and outward. Our present is our past. Therefore by studying our present we can learn much about our past. For example, if we meet someone and dislike them on sight it means that we have known and disliked them before, or we have known someone like them in a previous life and disliked that person. In either case, the present experience is a manifestation of the past.

10. And there is no beginning of them, the desire to live being eternal.

"Them" refers to samskaras and vasanas. As Taimni points out in his commentary, samskaras result the moment consciousness is touched by matter. By "matter" he means the subtlest of vibrations that are first encountered when the spirit-self begins to emerge into the realm of relativity and therefore relative experience. Yet before the emergence, or even the beginning of beginning, there cannot be samskaras because the spirit is untouched and therefore unconditioned. So this sutra cannot mean that samskaras are present with the spirit-self, because they have a beginning.

But we can say that they are potentially present in the sense of their possibility, because of *ashishah,* which *A Brief Sanskrit Glossary* defines as: "Primordial will; drive-to-survive; will-to-live; desire to live; expectation. From *a* which means near to or toward, and *shas* which means to order or direct. It is the force or impulse within the individual that causes it to pass from the absolute into the conditioned, from the transcendent into the immanent condition, from eternity into time, into relative existence."

Ashishah is the impulse to enter relativity. In *Robe of Light* I have written about it in this way: "All conscious beings have existed eternally within the being of God, the 'bosom of the Father' (John 1:18), living within the heart of God, one with him, distinct though not separate. Having their essential being rooted in the infinity of God, the individual consciousnesses have within them a natural impulse to transcend their finitude and attain the boundlessness of their Origin. This, of course, is impossible, since the essential, eternal nature of a being cannot be altered. Being rooted in God, and therefore in a sense a part of God, all beings are as immutable as God, the only infinite Being. Yet the urge for transcendence is part of their essential nature." And this urge for transcendence is ashishah which brings us into relative existence and ultimately out of it back into the transcendent state which is our original and ever-present state. For ashishah is eternal as an attribute of our very nature within the Absolute Being, within Satchidananda Brahman.

11. Being bound together as cause-effect, substratum-object, they [samskaras and vasanas] disappear on their [cause's] disappearance.

When the individual spirit-soul (atma) has fully run its course in the realm of evolutionary progress and has attained all that there is to attain, ashishah itself disappears, having been fulfilled by the age-long ascent up the evolutionary scale. Thus the individual spirit returns to its Source, leaving relative existence behind. If it so wills, it can return to relative existence but without any separation in consciousness from Satchidananda. In that state it will be an avatara, a descent of unalloyed consciousness into the realm of vibratory experience without losing its transcendent state.

12. The past and the future exist in their own [real] form. The difference of dharmas or properties is on account of the difference of paths [conditions].
13. They, whether manifest or unmanifest, are of the nature of Gunas.
14. The essence of the object consists in the uniqueness of transformation [of the Gunas].

These are very difficult sutras to explain, so much so that I put off doing so for a long time. The following points are made by them. In considering them we must realize that time is illusory. Otherwise it makes no sense at all.

1. Every action is a single vibrating thing, possessing past, present and future, and a dominant guna.
2. Past and future always exist. The past is not gone and the future is not yet to come, but are also present in the form of karma and samskara.
3. In action (karma) past, present and future are a single thing though their paths (modes of expression and manifestation) are different according to qualities or gunas which characterize the original action.
4. Sattwic actions have sattwic past and future, rajasic actions have rajasic past and future, and tamasic actions have tamasic past and future.
5. Therefore the effect of the past on the present, and the effect of both the past and present on the future vary according to the guna of the action.
6. The difference of the guna in these effects determine the path or mode in which they will influence or manifest.
7. The time of their influence or manifestation is also determined by the guna of the original action and the gunas that predominate

as the person moves from birth to birth, continually changing and hopefully evolving.

Practical summation: If a person can establish himself firmly in a single guna, then only the karmas and samskaras created by that guna can manifest–ever. For example, the yogi who establishes himself in sattwa guna will never undergo or experience the tamasic and rajasic karmas and samskaras. This is one of the ways the yogi snaps his karmic ties or destinies. Since sattwa tends ever upwards, the karmas and samskaras of the sattwic person will carry him upward and onward toward Self-realization, attaining which will annihilate all karmas and samskaras and set him free, establishing him in the eternal Now of Spirit.

15. The object being the same the difference in the two [the object and its cognition] are due to their [of the mind's] separate path.

Just as everyone knows that no two people see everything alike, in the same way each mind perceives its karmic objects totally according to the predominating guna of its present development. Therefore what will arise as object and the cognition of that object will depend totally on the present guna predominating in the individual's mind. Again, since the manifestation of karma also depends on the predominate guna, the cultivation of sattwa guna can lead to the dissolution of tamasic and rajasic karmas.

16. Nor is an object dependent on one mind. What would become of it when not cognized by that mind?

Strange as it has always seemed to me, there are some people who believe that the world exists only in their mind, and that when they cease to perceive it, it no longer exists. It certainly is true that our personal perception of the world is only in our mind, but that is a different matter altogether, and it does not imply that the world is unreal. Of course we have all encountered the question: "If a tree falls in the forest and there is no one around to hear it, does it make a sound?" And of course it does, because what we call "sound" is really vibrations in the air that we perceive (hear) as an auditory phenomenon. Those vibrations are made by the falling tree, no matter who is or is not around. That is like asking: "If the sun sets and no one sees it, has the sun not set?" Obviously when no one is around to see the Eiffel Tower it exists anyway.

Proof of the unity of God (Ishwara), the individual spirits (jivas) and the world (jagat) is the fact that they can share exact information about their experiences and have them verified by others. Everyone finds Chicago on the south shore of Lake Michigan and the Lake itself in the north central area of the United States, which we all certainly experience alike.

The question of "real" or "unreal" is another subject altogether: the nature of reality.

17. In consequence of the mind being colored or not colored by it, an object is known or unknown.

Alice Bailey: "These forms are cognized or not, according to the qualities latent in the perceiving consciousness."

Jnaneshwara Bharati: "Objects are either known or not known according to the way in which the coloring of that object falls on the coloring of the mind observing it."

The idea in all three of these translations is that an object is perceived by the mind (chitta) if the object and the mind are alike or compatible in vibration. If there is an affinity or similarity in the vibrations of the mind and an object, it is perceived; otherwise it is not. It is similar to the way that a magnet only picks up metals, and not all of them. As I say, there must be an affinity, a similarity between the two. This is why some experiences remain as vivid memory in some minds while others only recall them vaguely or even not at all. This is also why a person believes some things and disbelieves others. For example, an idea will be accepted by a mind that vibrates sympathetically with it, but is rejected or not even noticed or given consideration by a mind that does not vibrate in sympathy with it. This is why negative, deluded people readily believe lies and cling to them, and positive people respond only to the truth when they encounter it.

This is especially true in religion. Only what has a similar vibration to an individual's mind is accepted, and what has a dissimilar vibration is rejected. This is why so many people turn off their minds when entering the door of a church: They are not so stupid or negative as to believe the ludicrous and false beliefs of that church, but they want to be members. So they turn off their minds and never really attend with full intellectual attention. Evil, false and stupid religion attracts evil, false and stupid people. Intelligent, positive and true religion attracts intelligent, positive and genuine people. Those who do not believe in God or spiritual philosophies are those in which their own divine nature and spirituality are dead or dormant. Those who are alive in spirit believe in and are interested in spiritual things and those who are dead in spirit believe and are interested only in material things. Those of a subtle mind like subtle ideas; those of a coarse, simplistic mind like crude, obvious and simple ideas.

Sri Ramakrishna often said: "The mind is everything," and that is very true. Just as we are known by the kind of friends we have and the company we keep, so we are known by our mental character and the quality of our thoughts.

18. The modifications of the mind are always known to its lord on account of the changelessness of the purusha.

Jnaneshwara Bharati: "The activities of the mind are always known by the pure consciousness, because that pure consciousness is superior to, support of, and master over the mind."

Swami Prabhavananda: "Because the Atman, the Lord of the mind, is unchangeable, the mind's fluctuations are always known to it."

As said several times already, when asked: "What is the Self?" Sri Ramakrishna answered: "The witness of the mind." The mind is ever-changing in its impressions and projections, but the purusha, the Self, never changes, therefore it is impossible for it not to witness all the changes of the mind.

The continuity of experience and memory proves the existence of the witness-Self, that behind the body and mind is a conscious witness, the immortal, eternal spirit-Self of each one of us.

19. Nor is it self-illuminative, for it is perceptible.

Alice Bailey: "Because it can be seen or cognized it is apparent that the mind is not the source of illumination [perception]."

The mind is not conscious of itself, for its nature is not consciousness, but vibration: subtle matter (energy, actually). But even if it could be conscious, the witness of the mind–the consciousness of consciousness–would still be perceived behind it and accepted by the inquiring intelligence.

20. Moreover, it is impossible for it to be of both ways [as perceiver and perceived] at the same time.

The sense of smell cannot smell itself, the sense of taste cannot taste itself, the sense of sight cannot see itself, the sense of touch cannot touch itself, and the sense of hearing cannot hear itself. Yet some thing does indeed experience smell, taste, see, touch and hear. ("I smell, I taste, I see, I touch and I hear.") And that is the spirit-Self, the purusha.

21. If cognition of one mind by another [be postulated] we would have to assume cognition of cognitions and confusion of memories also.

Pandit Usharbudh Arya: "(If it were suggested) that (the mind) is the object of perception of another mind, then (the argument will suffer) a fallacious stretch (ad infinitum) so as (there will have to be) another buddhi for that buddhi (and for that buddhi, another and so on). Also (there will be) confusion of memories (as to which memory is of which buddhi)." This is the best summation possible.

22. Knowledge of its own nature through self-cognition [is obtained] when consciousness assumes that form in which it does not pass from place to place.

Bailey: "When the spiritual intelligence which stands alone and freed from objects, reflects itself in the mind stuff, then comes awareness of the Self."

Satchidananda: "The consciousness of the Purusha is unchangeable; by getting the reflection of it, the mind-stuff becomes conscious of the Self."

As you see, Bailey and Satchidananda consider that this verse is about the Self, the Purusha, becoming reflected in the mind which then becomes aware of the existence of the Self. There is a value to this for the yogi. The mind is vibrating energy which is drawn from the food the yogi eats, as the Chandogya Upanishad teaches. "That which is the subtlest part of curds rises, when they are churned and becomes butter. In the same manner that which is the subtlest part of the food that is eaten rises and becomes mind. Thus the mind consists of food" (Chandogya Upanishad 6.6.1, 2, 5). "Now is described the discipline for inner purification by which self-knowledge is attained: When the food is pure, the mind becomes pure. When the mind is pure the memory [smriti–memory of our eternal spirit-Self] becomes firm. When the memory is firm all ties are loosened" (Chandogya Upanishad 7.26.2). So right diet is necessary for success in yoga.

Vyas Houston: "The unchanging awareness [of purusha, the self] has an experience of its buddhi-function of cognition, upon the appearance of a form in that [chitta-field]."

Prabhavananda: "The pure consciousness of the Atman is unchangeable. As the reflection of its consciousness falls upon the mind, the mind takes the form of the Atman and appears to be conscious."

Houston and Prabhavananda interpret this sutra as being about the way the pure consciousness of the Self perceives the mind.

In my opinion, Taimni alone grasps the import of this sutra, so I am putting his comments here for you.

> "If cognition takes place through the agency of the mind and in the subtlest cognitions pertaining to the deepest levels of the mind we can know only the mind thus illuminated by consciousness, the question naturally arises "How are we to know consciousness itself or that light which illuminates the mind at all its levels?" The answer to this important question is given in the *Sutra* under discussion, but before we can understand its meanings it is necessary to consider carefully the various expressions used in it.
>
> *"Citeh* means "of consciousness" and is derived from *Citi* and not *Citta* which means the mind. *Apratisamkramayah* means "not passing from one to another", i.e. not passing from one level of *Citta* to another or from one vehicle to another. In *Samadhi* consciousness passes from one level of *Citta* to another and the phrase refers to the stage when this process stops or is brought to its limit. *Tad-akarapattau* means "on the accomplishment or assumption of its own form". Consciousness normally functions through the mind. This phrase refers to the condition in which it is freed from the limitations of the mind and is functioning in its own form. *Sva-buddhi* means *Buddhi* as it really is and not as it functions through the medium of the mind. We know only this function of perception as it appears in association with *Citta*. *Sva-buddhi* is the function of perception as it is when exercised upon itself. *Samvedanam* means "knowing of". Knowing is really a function of consciousness but when exercised through the mind becomes knowing something outside or external to pure consciousness. The phrase *Sva-buddhi*-samvedanam therefore means the knowledge which results when the faculty of *Buddhi* is turned upon itself. Normally, *Buddhi* functions through *Citta*

and helps the mind to perceive and understand objects in its realm. But when it is freed from the association of *Citta* it automatically turns upon itself and illuminates its own nature, i.e. consciousness. It is because the power of illumination is inherent in it that it illuminates *Citta* when it functions through *Citta*. If a light is enclosed within a translucent globe it reveals the globe. If the globe is removed the light reveals itself. From the meanings and explanations of the different phrases given above the inner significance of the *Sutra* should now be quite clear. *Buddhi*, as has been pointed out before, is that faculty which enables the mind to perceive and understand objects in the phenomenal worlds, the mind being inert and incapable of performing this function. As long as *Buddhi* is functioning through the medium of the mind it is not possible to know pure consciousness. It is only when it assumes that form in which all movement from one level of *Citta* to another has been eliminated that it reveals its real nature. As has been pointed out before, *Citta* or the mind has many levels corresponding to the different vehicles of consciousness and in *Samadhi* consciousness moves up and down from one level to another between the centre and periphery. In this kind of movement of consciousness there is no movement in space but only movement in different dimensions, the centre from which consciousness functions always remaining the same. When consciousness, in the state of *Samadhi*, has penetrated into the deepest level of *Citta* and then finally transcended even this level it is quite free from the limiting and obscuring action of *Citta* and it is only then that its true nature is realized. In this state the perceiver, perceived and perception all merge into one Self-illuminated Reality. So the answer to the question "How are we to know consciousness itself?" is "By diving in *Samadhi* into our consciousness until the mind in its subtlest form is transcended and the Reality hidden beneath it is revealed."

"From what has been said above it is apparent that we cannot understand the real nature of consciousness by applying the ordinary methods of modern psychology. What is known as consciousness in terms of modern psychology is only consciousness veiled by many layers of the mind, each of which increasingly obscures and modifies its nature as it infiltrates into the outermost physical mechanism, namely, the human brain. We thus observe consciousness in its ordinary manifestations through the physical brain under the greatest possible limitations and it is not possible to form any idea with regard to its true nature from these extremely partial and distorted manifestations. As well might a person who had always lived in a dungeon situated in a land where it was perpetually cloudy, try to form an idea regarding the light of the Sun from the gloom in which he lived. It will be seen, therefore, that not only is it impossible to know the true nature of consciousness by adopting the ordinary means available to the modern psychologist but also that the only effective means of doing so is to adopt the Yogic method. This is a subjective method, no doubt, and beyond the capacity of the ordinary man but it is the only method available. No amount of dissection of the brain and the nervous systems and study of human behaviour can unravel for us the mystery of consciousness itself. A great deal of research in this field of psychology is being carried on in very imposing laboratories in the West, a vast amount of so-called scientific data is being accumulated but all this effort is bound to prove futile from the very nature of the problem being tackled. The modern craze of submitting everything to physical examination may succeed with physical things but no physical instruments can ever be devised which will reveal the nature of consciousness which is of the nature of Spirit. All this waste of effort can be avoided and the whole field of modern psychology illuminated in the most effective manner if the facts of Yogic philosophy are properly understood and used in the study of psychological problems."

As you see, he considers that this sutra is about how both the mind and the Self become aware of one another. It is actually quite simple. When the consciousness that is the Self no longer experiences change or shifting from one object to another, but rests in its own pure nature, then it knows the mind because the mind then becomes absorbed into it and "becomes" the Self since it has never been anything other than the Self, for only the Self exists, the mind being its projection or dream-idea. So Sri Ramana Maharshi taught, and Taimni agrees, stating: "This is a subjective method, no doubt, and beyond the capacity of the ordinary man but it is the only method available."

Having laid the groundwork for the remaining sutras, Patanjali will now discuss what happens as the mind is being incrementally absorbed back into the Self.

23. The mind colored by the Knower [i.e., the Purusha] and the Known is all-apprehending.

Bailey: "Then the mind stuff, reflecting both the knower and the knowable, becomes omniscient."

Dwivedi: "The mind tinged by the seer and the seen has everything for its subject [of cognition]."

Jnaneshwara Bharati: "Therefore, the mind field, which is colored by both seer and seen, has the potential to perceive any and all objects."

Satchidananda: "The mind-stuff, when colored by both Seer and seen, understands everything."

The yogi eventually comes to participate in the omniscience, omnipresence and omnipotence of the Supreme. If he so desires, he is able to retain this state even in liberation or to drop even that and pass into his primal condition which has now been transmuted into something that cannot be conceived or spoken of. We can only know it is possible.

24. Though variegated by innumerable Vasanas it [the mind] acts for another [the purusha] for it acts in association.

Feuerstein and Houston use the terms "collaborate" and "collaboration" in the translations, conveying the idea that the transmuting mind becomes capable of functioning for the Self, as in the case of great teachers who become in a sense the messengers or spokesmen for God (Ishwara). In other words, a yogi in this state acts on behalf of God and is literally a mediator between God and humanity, just as Christianity originally understood about Jesus, though in time it fell into the error of believing that Jesus was unique in his mediatorship.

The great masters draw on their past impressions and developments in the form of the vasanas and use them to convey the divine wisdom that is essentially beyond speech or conception. Thus they give as accurate an impression of the Gnosis as is possible, at the same time assuring their hearers that what they say is only approximate and not absolute truth. No worthy student of such a master can ever create a dogmatic system around his master's teaching. Those who do so are failures, not disciples. This is true of all traditions, not just of Christianity.

25. The cessation [of desire] for dwelling in the consciousness of Atma for one who has seen the distinction.

The awakening mind right away develops a desire, a yearning, to experience the Self. At first it may not realize that to experience the Self is to become the Self, to be withdrawn into the Self. This is the true Ascension into Heaven that many religious traditions speak of their founder or great teachers attaining. And when that is attained, then the desire for that divine condition is fulfilled and therefore ceases, the Reality of it remaining.

26. Then, verily, the mind is inclined towards discrimination and gravitating towards kaivalya.

Jnaneshwara Bharati: "Then the mind is inclined towards the highest discrimination, and gravitates towards absolute liberation."

Vivekananda: "Then, bent on discriminating, the mind attains the previous state preliminary to kaivalya."

The mind of the transmuting yogi begins to clear-sightedly sift through his experiences, impulses and insights, rightly affirming what is true and discarding what is false, unburdening itself from untold ages of delusions and misperceptions. This process accelerates as it continues until finally he is divested of all that hinders his assumption into Infinite Being.

27. In the intervals arise other pratyayas from the force of samskaras.

Jnaneshwara Bharati: "When there are breaks or breaches in that high discrimination, other impressions arise from the deep unconscious."

This is necessary, for the purifying mind must deliberately discard what it deliberately took upon itself in previous existences. This is the real Last Judgment. Paramhansa Yogananda explained that the book of Revelation is not a prophecy of world events, but a symbolic panorama of the process of enlightenment that each one undergoes in the attainment of liberation. Here is the picture of the transmutation the yogi undergoes after the long processes of purification earlier described in the Beloved Disciple's vision:

> "And I saw a great white throne, and him that sat on it, from whose face the earth and the heaven fled away; and there was found no place for them. And I saw the dead, small and great, stand before God; and the books were opened: and another book was opened, which is the book of life: and the dead were judged out of those things which were written in the books, according to their works. And the sea gave up the dead which were in it; and death and hell delivered up the dead which were in them: and they were judged every man according to their works. And death and hell were cast into the lake of fire. This is the second death. And whosoever was not found written in

the book of life was cast into the lake of fire. And I saw a new heaven and a new earth: for the first heaven and the first earth were passed away; and there was no more sea" (Revelation 20:11-15; 21:1).

And I saw a great white throne, and him that sat on it, from whose face the earth and the heaven fled away; and there was found no place for them. When the subtle life forces (pranas) of the yogi rise completely into the Sahasrara chakra, the head, the Self is revealed before which relativity melts away because there is no longer need for them. The yogi is independent of all save the Supreme Self in which he has existed eternally.

And I saw the dead, small and great, stand before God; and the books were opened: and another book was opened, which is the book of life: and the dead were judged out of those things which were written in the books, according to their works. The "dead" are the samskaras and vasanas from the yogi's dead past, and the opening of the books is the process of discrimination mentioned in sutra twenty-six.

And the sea gave up the dead which were in it; and death and hell delivered up the dead which were in them: and they were judged every man according to their works. And death and hell were cast into the lake of fire. This is the second death. And whosoever was not found written in the book of life was cast into the lake of fire. The mind, which is symbolized by water even in our own dreams, reveals everything hidden there as described in the twenty-seventh sutra. And the yogi's discrimination consigns them to oblivion, to annihilation, just as previously they consigned his awareness to oblivion of spiritual realities and the annihilation of his wisdom and discrimination that was struggling within him to come forth just as leaven expands the dough in which it is hidden. ("Another parable spake he unto them; The kingdom of heaven is like unto leaven, which a woman took, and hid in three measures of meal, till the whole was leavened" Matthew 13:33.)

And I saw a new heaven and a new earth: for the first heaven and the first earth were passed away; and there was no more sea. This is an imaging of the completed transmutation of the yogi in which the energy field we call the mind no longer exists because it no longer has a purpose. The evolutionary movement is no more, for the goal has been reached toward which it ever tended. As the Buddhist texts say of those who have attained Nirvana: "Birth is ended, the holy life fulfilled [has been lived], the task done. There is nothing further for this world."

28. Their removal like that of kleshas, as has been described.

In the Sadhana Pada, sutras ten, eleven and twenty-six, we are told that meditation and discrimination are the means to dissolve the kleshas, and Patanjali tells us it is the same for the various samskaras and vasanas (pratyayas).

29. In the case of one, who is able to maintain a constant state of Vairagya even towards the most exalted state of enlightenment and to exercise the highest kind of discrimination, follows dharma-megha-samadhi.

Here in another case in which Taimni alone knows what this means, mostly because he alone understands the meaning of dharma-megha-samadhi which results from unbroken desirelessness and discrimination in relation to enlightenment. Let me give you his words, for without them I would not have a clue and cannot honestly write as though from my own understanding.

> "The combined practice of Viveka Khyati and Para-Vairagya when continued for a long time reaches, by a process of mutual reinforcement, a tremendous degree of intensity and culminates ultimately in Dharma-Megha-*Samadhi*, the highest kind of Samadhi which burns up the seeds of Samskaras and unlocks the gates of the World of Reality in which the Purusha lives eternally.
>
> "Why this *Samadhi* is called Dharma-Megha-Samadhi is not generally understood and the statements usually made are

forced explanations which do not make sense. In most of these explanations the word Dharma is interpreted as virtue or merit and Dharma-Megha is taken to mean "a cloud which showers virtues or merit" which, of course, explains nothing.

"The significance of the phrase Dharma-Megha will become clear if we assign to the word Dharma the meaning which it has in IV-12, namely that of property, characteristic or function. Megha, of course, is a technical term used in Yogic literature for the cloudy or misty condition through which consciousness passes in the critical state of Asamprajnata *Samadhi* when there is nothing in the field of consciousness.

"...the consciousness of the Yogi is trying to free itself from the last veil of illusion to emerge into the Light of Reality itself. When this effort succeeds the consciousness of the Yogi leaves the world of manifestation in which Gunas and their peculiar combinations, namely, Dharmas, operate and emerges into the world of Reality in which they no longer exist. His condition may be compared to the condition of a pilot in an airplane who comes out of a cloud bank into bright sunlight and begins to see everything clearly. Dharma-Megha-*Samadhi*, therefore, means the final Samadhi in which the Yogi shakes himself free from the world of Dharmas which obscure Reality like a cloud.

"The passage through Dharma-Megha-Samadhi completes the evolutionary cycle of the Individual.... No more can Avidya again obscure the vision of the Purusha who has attained full Self-realization. This process is irreversible and after reaching this stage it is not possible for the Purusha to fall again into the realm of Maya from which he has obtained Liberation. Before this final goal was reached it was possible for the Yogi to fall even from a very high stage of enlightenment, but not after he has passed through Dharma-Megha-Samadhi and attained the Enlightenment of Kaivalya.

> "The next five Sutras merely describe the results of passing through Dharma-Megha-Samadhi and attaining Kaivalya. It should be noted here that no effort is made to describe the experience of Reality. That would be futile for no one can imagine the transcendent glory of that consciousness into which the Yogi passes on attaining Kaivalya."

That Taimni was a yogi of the highest attainments we cannot doubt. Yet he travelled in obscurity through the world teaching the science of yoga to students who likewise practiced in obscurity–as did the sages and seekers of ancient India, in contrast to the usual situation today.

30. Then follows freedom from kleshas and karmas.

No need to comment on this except to refresh the memory of what klesha and karma really mean here. *A Brief Sanskrit Glossary* tells us:

Klesha: Literally, taints or afflictions. The kleshas are: ignorance, egotism, attractions and repulsions towards objects, and desperate clinging to physical life from the fear of death. (See Yoga Sutras 2:2-9.)

Karma: Karma, derived from the Sanskrit root *kri*, which means to act, do, or make, means any kind of action, including thought and feeling. It also means the effects of action. Karma is both action and reaction, the metaphysical equivalent of the principle: "For every action there is an equal and opposite reaction." "Whatsoever a man soweth, that shall he also reap" (Galatians 6:7). It is karma operating through the law of cause and effect that binds the jiva or the individual soul to the wheel of birth and death.

There are three forms of karma: sanchita, agami, and prarabdha. Sanchita karma is the vast store of accumulated actions done in the past, the fruits of which have not yet been reaped. Agami karma is the action that will be done by the individual in the future. Prarabdha karma is the action that has begun to fructify, the fruit of which is being reaped in this life.

31. Then, in consequence of the removal of all obscuration and impurities, that which can be known [through the mind] is but little in comparison with the infinity of knowledge [obtained in enlightenment].

Prabhavananda: "Then the whole universe, with all its objects of sense-knowledge, becomes as nothing in comparison to the infinite knowledge which is free from all obstruction and impurities."

Only those with this state of enlightenment are worthy of our attention and acceptance. Knowing the small value of the understanding of a mind still immersed in samsara, trustworthy teachers do not waste the time of their students with endless cosmologies, mythologies and all the other "ologies" that so fascinate the intellect of the ignorant and egotistical who have no real interest in liberation. Yogiraj Shyama Charan Lahiri is the ideal example of such a teacher. He spoke little, taught little, but revealed everything to those who sought worthily. It is the same with all authentic masters who alone are the true jnanis. Here, too, we see the valued example of Taimni.

32. The three gunas having fulfilled their object, the process of change [in the gunas] comes to an end.

Embodying that Self which is trigunatita, beyond the three gunas, the enlightened sage no longer experiences their permutations. It is not that the gunas remain in a kind of suspended or discarded state, but that they no longer exist for the liberated person who now experiences the world as the manifestation of consciousness, not energies such as the gunas.

33. The process, corresponding to moments which become apprehensible at the final end of transformation [of the gunas], is krama.

Krama means order; sequence; sequential order or progression; stage; underlying process; natural law–all these are inherent in their substratum or dharmi. There is the term krama-mukti, which means attainment of liberation in stages; gradual liberation; passing from this world to a higher world beyond rebirth and from there attaining liberation.

If we travel along a narrow track, we see but little of it, especially if we spend a long time in traversing it. But if we are suddenly lifted up as in helicopter, we will see its complete extent and its windings and dipping downs. In the same way, we encounter each state along the evolutionary path one at a time, each stage filling our consciousness completely, one after another, so we are absorbed in the moment. But when liberation is attained, in the final moments we see the entire extent, the path along which we have come to reach that moment of ending. Buddha tells us that all of our incarnations are clearly remembered in that moment and become present to us like the final answer of a complex mathematical problem. We see all that occurred in between the beginning and the end.

We will see that all was according to divine law, to the divine plan, that nothing occurred by chance but by the ever-present law of karma. And that everything took place by that precise laws of the interaction of the elements that comprised the vast chain of our lives within samsara.

34. Kaivalya is the state [of enlightenment] following re-mergence of the gunas because of their becoming devoid of the object of the purusha. In this state the purusha is established in his real nature which is pure consciousness.

Jnaneshwara Bharati: "When those primary elements involve, or resolve themselves back into that out of which they emerged, there comes liberation, wherein the power of pure consciousness becomes established in its true nature."

Taimni says that the meaning of this final sutra, simply put, is: "Kaivalya is that state of Self-realization in which the Purusha gets established finally when the purpose of his long evolutionary unfoldment has been attained. In this state the Gunas, haying fulfilled their purpose, recede to a condition of equilibrium and therefore the power of pure Consciousness can function without any obscuration or limitation."

What causes the remerging of the gunas into their original undifferentiated state? *The liberation of the individual purusha itself.* This is because the entire drama of entry into samsara and evolution out of samsara takes place solely in the consciousness of the individual. It is a dream within the greater dream of the universe. Ishwara dreams, and we dream inside his dream. It is all an exercise in the development (evolution) of consciousness. Material existence is a dream, a mirage, a kind of educational film brought before us for our learning and mastery.

Then the individual (jiva) is only what he was before this all began, but with an ineffable difference that is produced by its return to the depths of Original Being. The spirit is unchanged, yet somehow different. How so? It may be because of the effect of the dream. But whose dream? That of the individual or that of Ishwara? Ultimately, a yogi simply does not care, but bends all his powers to attain liberation. Then he will comprehend it all. And until we reach that state it is a waste of time for us try and understand. As Yogananda wrote in a chant: "He who knows–he knows. None else knows."

Note to the reader: This simple commentary on the Yoga Sutras is now finished. I hope it made them easier to understand.

Please obtain and study *The Science of Yoga* by I. K. Taimni. I have written this brief commentary in hope that you will be interested in learning so much more than I have conveyed in it. And that so much more is to be found in Taimni's commentary.

Then I urge you to read *Shankara on the Yoga Sutras: A Full Translation of the Newly Discovered Text*, by Trevor Leggett. It is not a perfect translation, but the only one currently available. The insights of Shankara and Vyasa that are found there are indispensible for the yogi's comprehension of Patanjali's actual meaning.

But the main indispensible is your own practice of yoga sadhana.

Did you enjoy reading this book?

Thank you for taking the time to read *Yoga: Science of the Absolute.* If you enjoyed it, please consider telling your friends or posting a short review at Amazon.com, Goodreads, or the site of your choice.

Word of mouth is an author's best friend and much appreciated.

Get your FREE Meditation Guide

Sign up for the Light of the Spirit Newsletter and get *Ten Simple Tips to Improve Your Meditation Today.*

Get free updates: newsletters, blog posts, and podcasts, plus exclusive content from Light of the Spirit Monastery.

Visit: http://ocoy.org/newsletter-registration

GLOSSARY

Abhimata: Desired; favorite; attractive; agreeable, appealing; object of choice.

Abhinivesha: Will to live; strong desire; false identification of the Self with the body or mind; an instinctive clinging to life and a dread of death.

Abhyantara: Internal; inward.

Abhyasa: Sustained spiritual practice.

Abhyasa Yoga: Yoga, or union with God, through sustained spiritual practice.

Adhyatma: The individual Self; the supreme Self; spirit.

Advaita: Non-dualism; non-duality; literally: not [a] two [dvaita].

Agami karma: The action that will be done by the individual in the future.

Ahimsa: Non-injury in thought, word, and deed; non-violence; non-killing; harmlessness.

Aishwarya: Dominion, power; lordship; divine glory; majesty; splendor; attribute(s) of Ishwara.

Akasha: Ether; space; sky; literally: "not visible." The subtlest of the five elements (panchabhuta), from which the other four arise. It is all-pervading, and is sometimes identified with consciousness–chidakasha. It is the basis of sound (shabda), which is its particular property.

Aklishta: Unafflicted; non-afflicted; unmoved.

Alabdhabhumikatva: Non-achievement of a stage; inability to find a footing.

Alasya: Laziness; idleness; apathy; sloth.

Alinga: Without any attribute, characteristic or mark; Parabrahman; noumenal; undifferentiated prakriti.

Ananda: Bliss; happiness; joy. A fundamental attribute of Brahman, which is Satchidananda: Existence, Consciousness, Bliss.

Anandamaya kosha: "The sheath of bliss (ananda)." The causal body. The borderline of the Self (atman).

Anandamayi Ma: One of the major spiritual figures in twentieth-century India, first made known to the West by Paramhansa Yogananda in his *Autobiography of a Yogi*.

Ananta: Infinite; without end; endless; a name of Shesha, the chief of the Nagas, whose coils encircle the earth and who symbolizes eternity, and upon whom Vishnu reclines.

Anatma(n): Not-Self; insentient.

Anavashtitatvani: Unsteadiness; instability of mind; inability to find a footing; mental unsteadiness.

Angamejayatva: Shaking of the body; lack of control over the body.

Anitya: Impermanent; transient.

Anubhava: Perception; direct personal experience; spiritual experience; intuitive consciousness and knowledge.

Anukarah: Following; imitating.

Anumana: Inference.

Aparigraha: Non-possessiveness, non-greed, non-selfishness, non-acquisitiveness.

Apavarga: Liberation; release; escape from pain; release from the bondage of embodiment.

Apunya: Demerit; vice; non-meritorious acts; unvirtuous deeds; sinful. See Punya.

Arjuna: The great disciple of Krishna, who imparted to him the teachings found in the Bhagavad Gita. The third of the Pandava brothers who were major figures in the Mahabharata War. His name literally means "bright," "white," or "clear."

Asamprajñata samadhi: Highest superconscious state where the mind and the ego-sense are completely annihilated.

Asamprayoga: Withdrawal of the senses from their objects; non-communication; non-interchange; withdrawal; disuniting; disconnecting.

Asana: Posture; seat; meditation posture; Hatha Yoga posture.

Ashaucha: Impurity; uncleanness.

Ashishah: Primordial will; drive-to-survive; will-to-live; desire to live; expectation. From *a* which means near to or toward, and *shas* which means to order or direct. It is the force within the individual that causes it to pass from the absolute into the conditioned, from the transcendent into the immanent condition, from eternity into time, into relative existence.

Asmita: I-ness; the sense of "I am;" "I exist;" sense of individuality.

Asteya: Non-stealing; honesty; non-misappropriativeness.

Atma(n): The individual spirit or Self that is one with Brahman. The true nature or identity.

Atmajnana: Knowledge of the Self.

Atmic: Having to do with the atma–spirit or self.

Aum: Alternate spelling of Om.

Avidya: Ignorance; nescience; unknowing; literally: "to know not." Also called ajnana.

Avirati: Hankering after objects; non-dispassion; sensual indulgence; lack of control; non-restraint.

Bahya: External; outward.

Bandha: "Lock;" bond; bondage; tie or knot.

Bhagavad Gita: "The Song of God." The sacred philosophical text often called "the Hindu Bible," part of the epic Mahabharata by Vyasa; the most popular sacred text in Hinduism.

Bhakti: Devotion; dedication; love (of God).

Bhakti Marga: The path of devotion leading to union with God.

Bhakti Sutra: An aphoristic work on devotional Yoga authored by the sage Narada. Another text by the same title is ascribed to the sage Shandilya.

Bhakti Yoga: The yoga of attaining union with God through the prescribed spiritual discipline of the path of devotion.

Bhakti Yogi: One who practices Bhakti Yoga.

Bhava: Subjective state of being (existence); attitude of mind; mental attitude or feeling; state of realization in the heart or mind.

Bhavamukha: An exalted state of spiritual experience, in which the aspirant keeps his mind on the borderline between the Absolute and the Relative. From this position he can contemplate the ineffable and attributeless Brahman and also participate in the activities of the relative world, seeing in it the manifestation of God alone.

Bhavanam: Meditation. "Bhavanam is setting the heart on the Lord Who is designated by Om and brought into the mind by It" (Shankara, Commentary on the Yoga Sutras). It has the connotation of all the awareness becoming focused and absorbed in it.

Bhaya: Fear; terror.

Bhoga: Enjoyment, pleasure; experience; perception; also food (usually what has been offered to a deity).

Bhranti: Delusion; wrong notion; false idea or impression.

Bhuta: What has come into being; an entity as opposed to the unmanifested; any of the five elementary constituents of the universe; element.

Bija: Seed; source.

Bija Mantra: A "seed" mantra from which realization grows as a tree from a seed; usually a single-syllable mantra.

Brahma: The Creator (Prajapati) of the three worlds of men, angels, and archangels (Bhur, Bhuwah, and Swah); the first of the created beings; Hiranyagarbha or cosmic intelligence.

Brahmachari: One who observes continence; a celibate student in the first stage of life (ashrama); a junior monk.

Brahmacharya: Continence; self-restraint on all levels; discipline; dwelling in Brahman.

Brahmajnana: Direct, transcendental knowledge of Brahman; Self-realization.

Brahman: The Absolute Reality; the Truth proclaimed in the Upanishads; the Supreme Reality that is one and indivisible, infinite, and eternal; all-pervading, changeless Existence; Existence-knowledge-bliss Absolute (Satchidananda); Absolute Consciousness; it is not only all-powerful but all-power itself; not only all-knowing and blissful but all-knowledge and all-bliss itself.

Brahmananda: The bliss of communion with Brahman.

Bhranti-darshana: Delusion; erroneous view.

Buddhi: Intellect; understanding; reason; the thinking mind; the higher mind, which is the seat of wisdom; the discriminating faculty.

Buddhi-sattwa: Experience of the buddhi in its most subtle level in which the buddhi and the Self are virtually indistinguishable; the experience of I-am (asmita/aham), experience of the Self through the buddhi.

Chaitanya: Consciousness; intelligence; awareness; the consciousness that knows itself and knows others; Pure Consciousness.

Chakra: Wheel. Plexus; center of psychic energy in the human system, particularly in the spine or head.

Chit: Consciousness (that is spirit or purusha); "to perceive, observe, think, be aware, know;" pure unitary Consciousness.

Chitshakti: Power of consciousness or intelligence.

Chitta: The subtle energy that is the substance of the mind, and therefore the mind itself; mind in all its aspects; the field of the mind; the field of consciousness; consciousness itself; the mind-stuff.

Chitta-vritti-nirodha: Cessation of the modifications of the mind; control of thoughts; Patanjali's definition of Yoga.

Darshan: Literally "sight" or "seeing;" vision, literal and metaphysical; a system of philosophy (see Sad-darshanas). Darshan is the seeing of a holy being as well as the blessing received by seeing such a one.

Darshana: "Seeing" in the sense of a viewpoint or system of thought. The Sad-darshanas are the six orthodox systems of Indian philosophy: Nyaya, Vaisheshika, Sankhya, Yoga, Mimamsa, and Vedanta.

Daurmanasya: Despair, depression etc., caused by mental sickness; feeling of wretchedness and miserableness.

Dayananda (Maharishi Swami): A leading reformer within Hinduism in the nineteenth century (1824-1883) and the founder of the Arya Samaj.

Desha: Place; locus; spot; space; country.

Deva: "A shining one," a god–greater or lesser in the evolutionary hierarchy; a semi-divine or celestial being with great powers, and therefore a "god." Sometimes called a demi-god. Devas are the demi-gods presiding over various powers of material and psychic nature. In many instances "devas" refer to the powers of the senses or the sense organs themselves.

Devata: Godhead; god; divinity; celestial being. See Deva.

Dharana: Concentration of mind; fixing the mind upon a single thing or point. "Dharana is the confining [fixing] of the mind within a point or area" (Yoga Sutras 3:1).

Dharma (1): The righteous way of living, as enjoined by the sacred scriptures and the spiritually illumined; characteristics; law; lawfulness; virtue; righteousness; norm.

Dharma (2): Attributes; natures; essential/visible characteristics; characteristic form; properties; qualifications.

Dharma-megha samadhi: The final state of one-pointedness, when an individual becomes disinterested even in omniscience, omnipotence, and omnipresence. This state of superconsciousness or samadhi is called dharma-megha–cloud of virtue–inasmuch as it showers nectar drops of immortality through knowledge of Brahman, when all the hosts of vasanas are entirely destroyed.

Dharmi (1): One who follows dharma.

Dharmi (2): The substratum in which attributes or characteristics are seen to manifest or inhere.

Dhyana(m): Meditation; contemplation.

Dirgha: Long; prolonged; protracted.

Divya: Divine; divine nature; heavenly; celestial; sacred; luminous; supernatural.

Drashta (1): Seer; perceiver; a title of both the individual and the Supreme Selves or Purushas.

Drishyam: The seen; the object seen; the seeable; visible; perceptible; object of consciousness; nature.

Dukha(m): Pain; suffering; misery; sorrow; grief; unhappiness; stress; that which is unsatisfactory.

Dwandwa(s): The pairs of opposites in nature (prakriti) such as pleasure and pain, hot and cold, light and darkness, gain and loss, victory and defeat, love and hatred.

Dwesha: Aversion/avoidance for something, implying a dislike for it. This can be emotional (instinctual) or intellectual. It may range from simple nonpreference to intense repulsion, antipathy and even hatred. See Raga.

Ganga: See Ganges.

Ganges (Ganga): The sacred river–believed to be of divine origin–that flows from high up in the Himalayas, through the plains of Northern India, and empties into the Bay of Bengal. Hindus consider that bathing in the Ganges profoundly purifies both body and mind.

Gita: Song; The Bhagavad Gita.

Gorakhnath/Gorakshanath: A master yogi of the Nath Yogi (Siddha Yogi) tradition. His dates are not positively known, but he seems to have lived for many centuries and travelled throughout all of India, Bhutan, Tibet, and Ladakh teaching philosophy and yoga.

Guna: Quality, attribute, or characteristic arising from nature (Prakriti) itself; a mode of energy behavior. As a rule, when "guna" is used it is in reference to the three qualities of Prakriti, the three modes of energy behavior that are the basic qualities of nature, and which determine the inherent characteristics of all created things. They are: 1) sattwa–purity, light, harmony; 2) rajas–activity, passion; and 3) tamas–dullness, inertia, and ignorance.

Himsa: Injury, violence; killing.

Hridaya: Heart; center or core of something; essence; the Self.

Indra: King of the lesser "gods" (demigods).

Indriya: Organ. The five organs of perception (jnanendriyas) are the ear, skin, eye, tongue, and nose. The five organs of action (karmendriyas) are the voice, hand, foot, organ of excretion, and the organ of generation.

Ishta-devata: Beloved deity. The deity preferred above all others by an individual. "Chosen ideal" is the usual English translation.

Ishta mantra: The mantra of the divine form specially beloved by an individual (ishta devata).

Ishwara: "God" or "Lord" in the sense of the Supreme Power, Ruler, Master, or Controller of the cosmos. "Ishwara" implies the powers of omnipotence, omnipresence, and omniscience.

Ishwarapranidhana: Offering of one's life to God (Ishwara).

Jada: Inert; unconscious; matter.

Jagadguru: "World guru;" world teacher.

Jagat: World; cosmos.

Janma: Birth; coming into being.

Japa: Repetition of a mantra.

Jati: Birth.

Jiva: Individual spirit.

Jivanmukta: One who is liberated here and now in this present life.

Jivanmukti: Liberation in this life.

Jivatma(n): Individual spirit; individual consciousness.

Jnana: Knowledge; knowledge of Reality–of Brahman, the Absolute; also denotes the process of reasoning by which the Ultimate Truth is attained. The word is generally used to denote the knowledge by which one is aware of one's identity with Brahman.

Jnanamaya kosha: "The sheath of intellect (buddhi)." The level of intelligent thought and conceptualization. Sometimes called the Vijnanamaya kosha. The astral-causal body.

Jnanendriya: The five organs of perception: ear, skin, eye, tongue, and nose.

Jnani: A follower of the path of knowledge (jnana); one who has realized–who knows–the Truth (Brahman).

Jnanopadesha: Instruction in wisdom (jnana).

Jyoti(h): Light; flame; illumination; luminosity; effulgence.

Jyotishmati: Effulgence; full of light.

Kala: Time measure, as in the time required to recite a mantra. It also sometimes means levels of creation or manifested beings.

Kailash(a): "Crystalline;" the name of the mountain home of Siva–a mountain peak in the Himalayas (in present-day Tibet) revered as the abode of Shiva, that is a famous place of pilgrimage.

Kaivalya: Transcendental state of Absolute Independence; state of absolute freedom from conditioned existence; moksha; isolation; final beatitude; emancipation.

Kaivalya-mukti: Liberation.

Kala: Time; a unit of time; part; aspect; bit; death (or Yama); fate; black.

Kapila: The great sage who formulated the Sankhya philosophy which is endorsed by Krishna in the Bhagavad Gita. (See the entry under Sankhya.)

Karana: "Instrument;" cause; instrumental cause; means of accomplishing something; reason. The means of knowledge and action. The inner and outer instruments (sense organs). The unmanifested potential cause that, in due time, takes shape as the visible effect;

the material cause of the universe in such a state during the period of dissolution, i.e., cosmic energy in a potential condition.

Karana sharira: The causal body (where the individual rests during sound, deep, dreamless sleep, the intellect, mind and senses being reduced to an unmanifested potential condition), also known as the anandamaya kosha, the "sheath of bliss."

Karika: Commentary; treatise.

Karmashaya: The receptacle or mass of karmas; aggregate of works done; latent impressions of action which will eventually fructify.

Karmendriya: The five organs of action: voice, hand, foot, organ of excretion, and the organ of generation.

Karmic: Having to do with karma.

Karuna: Mercy; compassion; kindness.

Kaupina: A small strip of cloth used to cover one's private parts. Also called a langoti.

Khyati: Apprehension; discernment; knowledge; vision.

Klesha: Literally, taints or afflictions. The kleshas are: ignorance, egotism, attractions and repulsions towards objects, and desperate clinging to physical life from the fear of death. (See Yoga Sutras 2:2-9.)

Klishta: Afflicted, painful or pain-bearing.

Kosha: Sheath; bag; scabbard; a sheath enclosing the soul; body. There are five such concentric sheaths or bodies: the sheaths of bliss, intellect, mind, life-force and the physical body–the anandamaya, jnanamaya, manomaya, pranamaya and annamaya bodies respectively.

Krama: Order; sequence; sequential order or progression; stage; underlying process; natural law–all these are inherent in their substratum or dharmi.

Krama-mukti: Attainment of liberation in stages; gradual liberation; passing from this world to a higher world beyond rebirth and from there attaining liberation.

Krishna: A Divine Incarnation born in India about three thousand years ago, Whose teachings to His disciple Arjuna on the eve of the Great India (Mahabharata) War comprise the Bhagavad Gita.

Kriya: Purificatory action, practice, exercise, or rite; action; activity; movement; function; skill. Kriyas purify the body and nervous system as well as the subtle bodies to enable the yogi to reach and hold on to higher levels of consciousness and being.

Kriya Yoga: The Yoga of Purification: "Austerity (tapasya), self-study (swadhyaya), and offering of the life to God (Ishwara pranidhana) are Kriya Yoga" (Yoga Sutras 2:1).

Krodha: Anger, wrath; fury.

Karma: Karma, derived from the Sanskrit root *kri*, which means to act, do, or make, means any kind of action, including thought and feeling. It also means the effects of action. Karma is both action and reaction, the metaphysical equivalent of the principle: "For every action there is an equal and opposite reaction." "Whatsoever a man soweth, that shall he also reap" (Galatians 6:7). It is karma operating through the law of cause and effect that binds the jiva or the individual soul to the wheel of birth and death. There are three forms of karma: sanchita, agami, and prarabdha. Sanchita karma is the vast store of accumulated actions done in the past, the fruits of which have not yet been reaped. Agami karma is the action that will be done by the individual in the future. Prarabdha karma is the action that has begun to fructify, the fruit of which is being reaped in this life.

Kumbhaka: Retention of breath; suspension of breath.

Lahiri Mahasaya: Shyama Charan Lahiri, one of the greatest yogis of nineteenth-century India, written about extensively in *Autobiography of a Yogi* by Paramhansa Yogananda.

Lila: Play; sport; divine play; the cosmic play. The concept that creation is a play of the divine, existing for no other reason than for the mere joy of it. The life of an avatar is often spoken of as lila.

Linga: Mark; gender; sign; symbol.

Lobha: Greed; covetousness.

Loka: World or realm; sphere, level, or plane of existence, whether physical, astral, or causal.

Mahapralaya: The final cosmic dissolution; the dissolution of all the worlds of relativity (Bhuloka, Bhuvaloka, Swaloka, Mahaloka, Janaloka, Tapaloka, and Satyaloka), until nothing but the Absolute remains. There are lesser dissolutions, known simply as pralayas, when only the first five worlds (lokas) are dissolved.

Maharshi: Maha-rishi–great sage.

Manas(a): The sensory mind; the perceiving faculty that receives the messages of the senses.

Mantra(m): Sacred syllable or word or set of words through the repetition and reflection of which one attains perfection or realization of the Self. Literally, "a transforming thought" (manat trayate). A mantra, then is a sound formula that transforms the consciousness.

Mantric: Having to do with mantra(s)–their sound or their power.

Manu: The ancient lawgiver, whose code, The Laws of Manu (Manu Smriti) is the foundation of Hindu religious and social conduct.

Marga: Way; path; street; approach to God-realization (bhakti marga, jnana marga, karma marga, yoga marga, etc.).

Maya: The illusive power of Brahman; the veiling and the projecting power of the universe, the power of Cosmic Illusion. "The Measurer"–a reference to the two delusive "measures," Time and Space.

Moha: Delusion–in relation to something, usually producing delusive attachment or infatuation based on a completely false perception and evaluation of the object.

Moksha: Release; liberation; the term is particularly applied to the liberation from the bondage of karma and the wheel of birth and death; Absolute Experience.

Mudita: Complacency; joy; happiness.

Mukta: One who is liberated–freed–usually in the sense of one who has attained moksha or spiritual liberation.

Mukti: Moksha; liberation.

Muni: "Silent one" (one observing the vow of silence (mauna); sage; ascetic.

Nadi: A channel in the subtle (astral) body through which subtle prana (psychic energy) flows; a physical nerve. Yoga treatises say that there are seventy-two thousand nadis in the energy system of the human being.

Nath(a): Lord; ruler; protector.

Nath Yogis: An ancient order of yogis, sometimes called Siddha Yogis, claiming Patanjali and Jesus (Isha Nath) among their master teachers.

Neem Karoli Baba: One of India's most amazing and mysterious spiritual figures. The life of this great miracle-worker and master spanned from two to four centuries (at the least), including most of the twentieth century.

Nidra: Sleep; either dreaming or deep sleep state.

Nirbija: "Without seed;" without attributes; without the production of samskaras or subtle karmas.

Nirbija samadhi: Nirvikalpa samadhi wherein the seeds of samskaras or karmas are destroyed ("fried" or "roasted") by Jnana, and which produces no samskaras or karmas.

Nirodha: Restraint; restriction; suppression; dissolving/dissolution; cessation; disappearance; control inhibition; annihilation; process of ending.

Nirvana: Liberation; final emancipation; the term is particularly applied to the liberation from the bondage of karma and the wheel of birth and death that comes from knowing Brahman; Absolute Experience. See Moksha.

Nirvichara samadhi: A stage in samadhi wherein the mind (chitta) no longer identified with a subtle object or assumes its form, simply resting in perception without analytical awareness of its nature by means of the buddhi, whose operation has become completely suspended so that only pure awareness remains; without deliberation and reasoning or inquiry.

Nirvikalpa: Indeterminate; non-conceptual; without the modifications of the mind; beyond all duality.

Nirvikalpa samadhi: Samadhi in which there is no objective experience or experience of "qualities" whatsoever, and in which the triad of knower, knowledge and known does not exist; purely subjective experience of the formless and qualitiless and unconditioned Absolute. The highest state of samadhi, beyond all thought, attribute, and description.

Nirvitarka samadhi: Union with an object in which remembrance of their names and qualities is not present. (See Vitarka.)

Nitya: Eternal; permanent; unchanging; the ultimate Reality; the eternal Absolute. Secondarily: daily or obligatory (nitya karma–that which must be done every day).

Nityananda (Paramhansa): A great Master of the nineteenth and twentieth centuries, and the most renowned So'ham yogi of our times. His Chidakasha Gita contains some of the most profound statements on philosophy and yoga.

Nivritti: Negation; the path of turning away from activity; withdrawal. Literally, "to turn back." The path of renunciation.

Niyama: Observance; the five Do's of Yoga: 1) shaucha–purity, cleanliness; 2) santosha–contentment, peacefulness; 3) tapas–austerity, practical (i.e., result-producing) spiritual discipline; 4) swadhyaya–self-study, spiritual study; 5) Ishwarapranidhana–offering of one's life to God.

Om: The Pranava or the sacred syllable symbolizing and embodying Brahman.

Omkara: Om.

Para(m): Highest; universal; transcendent; supreme.

Parabrahman: Supreme Brahman.

Paramatma(n): The Supreme Self, God.

Paramahan[m]sa/Paramhan[m]sa: Literally: Supreme Swan, a person of the highest spiritual realization, from the fact that a swan can separate milk from water and is therefore an apt symbol for one who has discarded the unreal for the Real, the darkness for the Light, and mortality for the Immortal, having separated himself fully from all that is not God and joined himself totally to the Divine, becoming a veritable embodiment of Divinity manifested in humanity.

Paramhansa Yogananda: The most influential yogi of the twentieth century in the West, author of *Autobiography of a Yogi* and founder of Self-Realization Fellowship in America.

Parashakti: Supreme Power.

Parinama: Change; modification; transformation; evolution; development; effect; result; ripening; altering/changing.

Patanjali: A yogi of ancient India, the author of the Yoga Sutras.

Pinda: Part of the whole; individual; the body–either of the individual jiva or the cosmic body of Ishwara. It can also mean an organized whole or a unity of diversities.

Pitri: A departed ancestor, a forefather.

Pradhana: Prakriti; causal matter.

Prajapati: Progenitor; the Creator; a title of Brahma the Creator.

Prajna: Consciousness; awareness; wisdom; intelligence.

Prajapati: Progenitor; the Creator; a title of Brahma the Creator.

Prakash(a): Shining; luminous; effulgence; illumination; luminosity; light; brightness. Pure Consciousness, from the root kash (to shine) and pra (forth); cognition.

Prakriti: Causal matter; the fundamental power (shakti) of God from which the entire cosmos is formed; the root base of all elements; undifferentiated matter; the material cause of the world. Also known as Pradhana. Prakriti can also mean the entire range of vibratory existence (energy).

Prakritilaya: Absorbed or merged in Prakriti; the state of yogis who have so identified with the cosmic energy that they are trapped in it as though in a net and cannot separate themselves from it and evolve onwards until the cosmic dissolution (pralaya) occurs in which the lower worlds of men, angels, and archangels (bhur, bhuwah and swar lokas) are dissolved.

Pramada: Carelessness; fault; guilt.

Pramana: Means of valid knowledge; logical proof; authority (of knowledge); means of cognition (from the verb root ma–to measure and pra–before or forward.

Prana: Life; vital energy; life-breath; life-force; inhalation. In the human body the prana is divided into five forms: 1) Prana, the prana that moves upward; 2) Apana: The prana that moves downward, producing the excretory functions in general. 3) Vyana: The prana that holds prana and apana together and produces circulation in the body. 4) Samana: The prana that carries the grosser material of food to the apana and brings the subtler material to each limb; the general force of digestion. 5) Udana: The prana which brings up or carries down what has been drunk or eaten; the general force of assimilation.

Pranamaya kosha: "The sheath of vital air (prana)." The sheath consisting of vital forces and the (psychic) nervous system.

Pranava: A title of Om, meaning "Life-ness" or "Life-Giver." Om is the expression or controller of prana–the life force within the individual being and the cosmos.

Pranayama: Control of the subtle life forces, often by means of special modes of breathing. Therefore breath control or breathing exercises are usually mistaken for pranayama. It also means the refining (making subtle) of the breath, and its lengthening through spontaneous slowing down of the respiratory rate.

Prarabdha: Karma that has become activated and begun to manifest and bear fruit in this life; karmic "seeds" that have begun to "sprout."

Prasad(am): Grace; food or any gift that has been first offered in worship or to a saint; that which is given by a saint. It also means tranquility, particularly in the Bhagavad Gita.

Pratibha: Special mental power; imaginative insight; intelligence; splendor of knowledge; intuition; ever-creative activity or consciousness; the spontaneous supreme "I"-consciousness; Parashakti.

Pratipaksha bhavana(m): The method of substituting the opposite through imagination; thus, fear is overcome by dwelling strongly upon its opposite, viz., courage. Reflecting on and cultivating those traits which are opposed to spiritual obstructions.

Pratyahara: Abstraction or withdrawal of the senses from their objects, the fifth limb of Patanjali's Ashtanga Yoga.

Pratyaksha: Perception; direct perception; intuition.

Pravritti: Action; endeavor. Literally: "to turn forth."

Pratyayau: Content of the mind-field; presented idea; cognition principle; cognition; causal/awareness principle; awareness perceiving [through the mind]; buddhi; discriminatory intelligence; immediate arising thought directed to an object; cause; mental effort; imagination; idea of distinction.

Punya: Merit; virtue; meritorious acts; virtuous deeds. See Apunya.

Puraka: Inhalation.

Purusha: "Person" in the sense of a conscious spirit. Both God and the individual spirits are purushas, but God is the Adi (Original, Archetypal) Purusha, Parama (Highest) Purusha, and the Purushottama (Highest or Best of the Purushas).

Purushottama: The Supreme Person; Supreme Purusha. (See Purusha.)

Raga: Attachment/affinity for something, implying a desire for it. This can be emotional (instinctual) or intellectual. It may range from simple liking or preference to intense desire and attraction. Greed; passion. See Dwesha.

Rajas: Activity, passion, desire for an object or goal.

Rajasic: Possessed of the qualities of the raja guna (rajas). Passionate; active; restless.

Ramakrishna, Sri: Sri Ramakrishna lived in India in the second half of the nineteenth century, and is regarded by all India as a perfectly enlightened person–and by many as an Incarnation of God.

Ramana Maharshi: A great sage of the twentieth century who lived in Arunachala in South India. He taught the path of Self-Inquiry (Atma Vichara) wherein the person simply turns his awareness within with the unspoken question–the attitude–of "Who am I?" until the self (atma) is revealed.

Rechaka: Exhalation of breath.

Rishi: Sage; seer of the Truth.

Rita(m): Truth; Law; Right; Order. The natural order of things, or Cosmic Order/Law. Its root is ri, which means "to rise, to tend upward." It is said to be the basis for the Law of Karma.

Rupa: Form; body.

Sabija: "With seed;" with attributes; producing samskaras or subtle karmas.

Sabija samadhi: Savikalpa samadhi wherein the seeds of samskaras or karmas are not destroyed, and which produces the highest and subtlest of samskaras or karmas.

Sadguru: True guru, or the guru who reveals the Real (Sat–God).

Sadhaka: One who practices spiritual discipline–sadhana–particularly meditation.

Sadhana: Spiritual practice.

Sadhu: Seeker for truth (sat); a person who is practicing spiritual disciplines. Usually this term is applied only to monastics.

Sahasrara: The "thousand-petalled lotus" of the brain. The highest center of consciousness, the point at which the spirit (atma) and the bodies (koshas) are integrated and from which they are disengaged.

Samadhana: Equal fixing; proper concentration; complete concentration; the root word of samadhi.

Samadhi: The state of superconsciousness where Absoluteness is experienced attended with all-knowledge and joy; Oneness; here the mind becomes identified with the object of meditation; the meditator and the meditated, thinker and thought become one in perfect absorption of the mind. See Samprajñata *Samadhi*, Asamprajñata *Samadhi*, Savikalpa *Samadhi*, and Nirvikalpa *Samadhi*.

Samana: The prana the carries the grosser material of food to the apana and brings the subtler material to each limb; the general force of digestion.

Samarasya: Homogeneity; oneness–especially of essence–which results from the elimination of all differences; equilibrium; the process of bringing the body into a harmonious resonance with the Divine.

Samprajñata samadhi: State of superconsciousness, with the triad of meditator, meditation and the meditated; lesser samadhi; cognitive samadhi; samadhi of wisdom; meditation with limited external awareness. Savikalpa samadhi.

Samsara: Life through repeated births and deaths; the wheel of birth and death; the process of earthly life.

Samshaya: Doubt; suspicion.

Samskara: Impression in the mind, either conscious or subconscious, produced by previous action or experience in this or previous lives; propensities of the mental residue of impressions; subliminal activators; prenatal tendency. See Vasana.

Samvega: Intense ardor derived from long practice.

Samvit: Knowledge; consciousness; awareness; intelligence; supreme consciousness.

Samyama: Self-control; perfect restraint; an all-complete condition of balance and repose. The combined practice of the last three steps in Patanjali's Ashtanga Yoga: concentration (dharana), meditation (dhyana), and union (samadhi). See the Vibhuti Pada of the Yoga Sutras.

Samyoga: Conjunction; contact.

Sanatana Dharma: "The Eternal Religion," also known as "Arya Dharma," "the religion of those who strive upward [Aryas]." Hinduism.

Sanchita karma: The vast store of accumulated actions done in the past, the fruits of which have not yet been reaped.

Sankhya: One of the six orthodox systems of Hindu philosophy whose originator was the sage Kapila, Sankhya is the original Vedic philosophy, endorsed by Krishna in the Bhagavad Gita (Gita 2:39; 3:3,5; 18:13,19), the second chapter of which is entitled "Sankhya Yoga." *A Ramakrishna-Vedanta Wordbook* says: "Sankhya postulates two ultimate realities, Purusha and Prakriti. Declaring that the cause of suffering is man's identification of Purusha with Prakriti and its products, Sankhya teaches that liberation and true knowledge are attained in the supreme consciousness, where such identification ceases and Purusha is realized as existing independently in its transcendental nature." Not surprisingly, then, Yoga is based on the Sankhya philosophy.

Sankhyabhih: Numbers.

Sanskrit: The language of the ancient sages of India and therefore of the Indian scriptures and yoga treatises.

Santosha: Contentment; peacefulness.

Sarva(m): All; everything; complete.

Sarvajña(twa): Knowing everything; omniscience.

Sat: Existence; reality; truth; being; a title of Brahman, the Absolute or Pure Being.

Satchidananda: Existence-Knowledge-Bliss Absolute; Brahman.

Satya(m): Truth; the Real; Brahman, or the Absolute; truthfulness; honesty.

Satya Loka: "True World," "World of the True [Sat]", or "World of Truth [Satya]." This highest realm of relative existence where liberated beings live who have not entered back into the Transcendent Absolute where there are no "worlds" (lokas). From that world they can descend and return to other worlds for the spiritual welfare of others, as can those that have chosen to return to the Transcendent.

Sattwa: Light; purity; harmony, goodness, reality.

Sattwa Guna: Quality of light, purity, harmony, and goodness.

Sattwic: Partaking of the quality of Sattwa.

Savichara samadhi: A stage in samadhi wherein the mind (chittta) is identified with some subtle object and assumes its form, being aware of what it is and capable of analyzing it by means of the purified buddhi; with deliberation and reasoning or inquiry.

Savikalpa Samadhi: Samadhi in which there is objective experience or experience of "qualities" and with the triad of knower, knowledge and known; lesser samadhi; cognitive samadhi; samadhi of wisdom; meditation with limited external awareness. Samprajñata samadhi.

Savitarka Samadhi: The union (samadhi) in which the mind concentrates on objects, remembering their names and qualities. (See Vitarka.)

Shabda: Sound; word.

Shakti: Power; energy; force; the Divine Power of becoming; the apparent dynamic aspect of Eternal Being; the Absolute Power or Cosmic Energy; the Divine Feminine.

Shankara: Shankaracharya; Adi (the first) Shankaracharya: The great reformer and re-establisher of Vedic Religion in India around 500 B.C. He is the unparalleled exponent of Advaita (Non-Dual) Vedanta. He also reformed the mode of monastic life and founded (or regenerated) the ancient Swami Order.

Shanta: One who possesses shanti.

Sharira: Body; sheath; literally: "that which perishes," from the root shri which means "to waste away."

Shastra: Scripture; spiritual treatise.

Shaucha: Purity; cleanliness.

Shiva: A name of God meaning "One Who is all Bliss and the giver of happiness to all." Although classically applied to the Absolute

Brahman, Shiva can also refer to God (Ishwara) in His aspect of Dissolver and Liberator (often mistakenly thought of as "destroyer").

Shraddha: Faith; confidence or assurance that arises from personal experience.

Shravana: Hearing; study; listening to reading of the scriptures or instruction in spiritual life.

Shrotra: Ear; the sense or faculty of hearing

Shuddha: Pure; clear; clean; untainted.

Shuddhi: The state of purity (shuddha); purification.

Shunya: Void; no-thing; emptiness.

Shvasa-prashvasa: Hard breathing; inspiration and expiration.

Shyama Charan Lahiri: See Lahiri Mahasaya.

Siddha: A perfected–liberated–being, an adept, a seer, a perfect yogi.

Siddhi: Spiritual perfection; psychic power; power; modes of success; attainment; accomplishment; achievement; mastery; supernatural power attained through mantra, meditation, or other yogic practices. From the verb root sidh–to attain.

Sivananda (Swami): A great twentieth-century Master, founder of the world-wide Divine Life Society, whose books on spiritual life and religion are widely circulated in the West as well as in India.

Smriti: Memory; recollection; "that which is remembered." In this latter sense, Smriti is used to designate all scriptures except the Vedas and Upanishads (which are considered of greater authority).

Sthiti: Steadiness; condition or state; existence; being; subsistence; preservation.

Sukha(m): Happiness; ease; joy; happy; pleasant; agreeable.

Sukshma: Subtle; fine.

Sukshma sharira: Subtle body; astral body (also called linga sharira).

Sushupti: The dreamless sleep state.

Sutra: Literally: a thread; an aphorism with minimum words and maximum sense; a terse sentence; in Buddhism, an entire scripture.

Swadhyaya: Introspective self-study or self-analysis leading to self-understanding. Study of spiritual texts regarding the Self.

Swapna: The dream state; a dream.

Swarupa: "Form of the Self." Natural–true–form; actual or essential nature; essence. A revelatory appearance that makes clear the true nature of some thing.

Taimni, I. K.: A professor of chemistry in India. He wrote many excellent books on philosophy and spiritual practice, including The Science of Yoga, a commentary on the Yoga Sutras. For many years he was the spiritual head of the Esoteric Section of the Theosophical Society headquartered in Adyar, Madras (Tamilnadu), and traveled the world without publicity or notoriety, quietly instructing many sincere aspirants in the path to supreme consciousness.

Tamas: Dullness, darkness, inertia, folly, and ignorance.

Tamasic: Possessed of the qualities of the tamo guna (tamas). Ignorant; dull; inert; and dark.

Tapas: See tapasya.

Tapasya: Austerity; practical (i.e., result-producing) spiritual discipline; spiritual force. Literally it means the generation of heat or energy, but is always used in a symbolic manner, referring to spiritual practice and its effect, especially the roasting of karmic seeds, the burning up of karma.

Taraka: Deliverer.

Trigunatita: Beyond the three gunas.

Tukaram: A poet-saint of seventeenth century India (Maharashtra) devoted to Krishna in his form of Panduranga (Vittala).

Turiya: The state of pure consciousness. *A Ramakrishna-Vedanta Wordbook* defines it as: "The superconscious; lit., 'the Fourth,' in relation to the three ordinary states of consciousness–waking, dreaming, and dreamless sleep–which it transcends."

Udana: The prana which brings up or carries down what has been drunk or eaten; the general force of assimilation.

Upanishads: Books (of varying lengths) of the philosophical teachings of the ancient sages of India on the knowledge of Absolute Reality. The upanishads contain two major themes: (1) the individual self (atman) and the Supreme Self (Paramatman) are one in essence, and (2) the goal of life is the realization/manifestation of this unity, the realization of God (Brahman). There are eleven principal upanishads: Isha, Kena, Katha, Prashna, Mundaka, Mandukya, Taittiriya, Aitareya, Chandogya, Brihadaranyaka, and Shvetashvatara, all of which were commented on by Shankara, Ramanuja and Madhavacharya, thus setting the seal of authenticity on them.

Upeksha[nam]: Indifference; equanimity resulting from disinterestedness.

Vachaka: That which is denoted by speech.

Vairagya: Non-attachment; detachment; dispassion; absence of desire; disinterest; or indifference. Indifference towards and disgust for all worldly things and enjoyments.

Vak: Speech.

Vasana: Subtle desire; a tendency created in a person by the doing of an action or by enjoyment; it induces the person to repeat the action or to seek a repetition of the enjoyment; the subtle impression in the mind capable of developing itself into action; it is the cause of birth and experience in general; the impression of actions that remains unconsciously in the mind.

Vasana(s): A bundle or aggregate of such samskaras.

Vasyata: Mastery; control; obedience.

Veda: Knowledge, wisdom, revealed scripture. See Vedas.

Vedanta: Literally, "the end of the Vedas;" the Upanishads; the school of Hindu thought, based primarily on the Upanishads, upholding the doctrine of either pure non-dualism or conditional non-dualism. The original text of this school is Vedanta-darshana, the Brahma Sutras compiled by the sage Vyasa.

Vedas: The oldest scriptures of India, considered the oldest scriptures of the world, that were revealed in meditation to the Vedic Rishis (seers). Although in modern times there are said to be four Vedas (Rig, Sama, Yajur, and Atharva), in the upanishads only three are listed (Rig, Sama, and Yajur). In actuality, there is only one Veda: the Rig Veda. The Sama Veda is only a collection of Rig Veda hymns that are marked (pointed) for singing. The Yajur Veda is a small book giving directions on just one form of Vedic sacrifice. The Atharva Veda is only a collection of theurgical mantras to be recited for the cure of various afflictions or to be recited over the herbs to be taken as medicine for those afflictions.

Vedic: Having to do with the Vedas.

Vibhuti: Manifestations of divine power or glory; might; prosperity; welfare; splendor; exalted rank; greatness; miraculous powers; superhuman power resembling that of God (Ishwara). The quality of all-pervasiveness (omnipresence).

Vichara: Subtle thought; reflection; enquiry; introspection; investigation; enquiry/investigation into the nature of the Self, Brahman or Truth; ever-present reflection on the why and wherefore of things; enquiry into the real meaning of the Mahavakya Tat-twam-asi: Thou art That; discrimination between the Real and the unreal; enquiry of Self.

Vidya: Knowledge; both spiritual knowledge and mundane knowledge.

Vijnana: The highest knowledge, beyond mere theoretical knowledge (jnana); transcendental knowledge or knowing; experiential knowledge; a high state of spiritual realization–intimate knowledge of God in which all is seen as manifestations of Brahman; knowledge of the Self.

Vikalpa: Imagination; fantasy; mental construct; abstraction; conceptualization; hallucination; distinction; experience; thought; oscillation of the mind.

Vikshepa: The projecting power of the mind, causing external involvement; the movement of pushing outward or away; the projecting power of ignorance; mental restlessness resulting from the awareness moving out from the center that is the Self; Distractions; causes of distractions; projection; false projection; the tossing of the mind which obstructs concentration.

Virya: Strength; power; energy; courage.

Vishuddha: Supremely pure; totally pure.

Vishuddha chakra: "Supreme purity." Energy center located in the spine opposite the hollow of the throat. Seat of the Ether element.

Vishwaprana: The universal life force (prana).

Vitarka: Thought; reasoning; cogitation with sense perception; discussion; debate; logical argument.

Viveka: Discrimination between the Real and the unreal, between the Self and the non-Self, between the permanent and the impermanent; right intuitive discrimination.

Vivekananda (Swami): The chief disciple of Sri Ramakrishna, who brought the message of Vedanta to the West at the end of the nineteenth century.

Vritti: Thought-wave; mental modification; mental whirlpool; a ripple in the chitta (mind substance).

Yantra: Geometrical designs of the energy patterns made by mantras when they are recited or which, when concentrated on produce the effects of the corresponding mantras. Though often attributed to deities, they are really the diagrams of the energy movements of those deities' mantras.

Yoga: Literally, "joining" or "union" from the Sanskrit root yuj. Union with the Supreme Being, or any practice that makes for such union. Meditation that unites the individual spirit with God, the Supreme Spirit. The name of the philosophy expounded by the sage Patanjali, teaching the process of union of the individual with the Universal Soul.

Yoga Darshana: See Yoga Sutras.

Yoga Sutras: The oldest known writing on the subject of yoga, written by the sage Patanjali, a yogi of ancient India, and considered the most authoritative text on yoga. Also known as Yoga Darshana, it is the basis of the Yoga Philosophy which is based on the philosophical system known as Sankhya.

Yogananda (Paramhansa): The most influential yogi of the twentieth century in the West, author of *Autobiography of a Yogi* and founder of Self-Realization Fellowship in America.

Yogi: One who practices Yoga; one who strives earnestly for union with God; an aspirant going through any course of spiritual discipline.

Yogic: Having to do with Yoga.

Yogiraj: "King of Yogis," a title often given to an advanced yogi, especially a teacher of yogi.

Yathartha: Real; a things as it really is.

ABOUT THE AUTHOR

Abbot George Burke (Swami Nirmalananda Giri) is the founder and director of the Light of the Spirit Monastery (Atma Jyoti Ashram) in Cedar Crest, New Mexico, USA.

In his many pilgrimages to India, he had the opportunity of meeting some of India's greatest spiritual figures, including Swami Sivananda of Rishikesh and Anandamayi Ma. During his first trip to India he was made a member of the ancient Swami Order by Swami Vidyananda Giri, a direct disciple of Paramhansa Yogananda, who had himself been given sannyas by the Shankaracharya of Puri, Jagadguru Bharati Krishna Tirtha.

In the United States he also encountered various Christian saints, including Saint John Maximovich of San Francisco and Saint Philaret Voznesensky of New York. He was ordained in the Liberal Catholic Church (International) to the priesthood on January 25, 1974, and consecrated a bishop on August 23, 1975.

For many years Abbot George has researched the identity of Jesus Christ and his teachings with India and Sanatana Dharma, including Yoga. It is his conclusion that Jesus lived in India for most of his life, and was a yogi and Sanatana Dharma missionary to the West. After his resurrection he returned to India and lived the rest of his life in the Himalayas.

He has written extensively on these and other topics, many of which are posted at OCOY.org.

Light of the Spirit Monastery

Light of the Spirit Monastery is an esoteric Christian monastic community for those men who seek direct experience of the Spirit through meditation, sacramental worship, discipline and dedicated communal life, emphasizing the inner reality of "Christ in you the hope of glory," as taught by the illumined mystics of East and West.

The public outreach of the monastery is through its website, OCOY.org (Original Christianity and Original Yoga).There you will find many articles on Original Christianity and Original Yoga, including *Esoteric Christian Beliefs. Foundations of Yoga* and *How to Be a Yogi* are practical guides for anyone seriously interested in living the Yoga Life.

You will also discover many other articles on leading an effective spiritual life, including *The Yoga of the Sacraments* and *Spiritual Benefits of a Vegetarian Diet*, as well as the "Dharma for Awakening" series–in-depth commentaries on these spiritual classics: the Upanishads, the Bhagavad Gita, the Dhammapada, and the Tao Teh King.

You can listen to podcasts by Abbot George on meditation, the Yoga Life, and remarkable spiritual people he has met in India and elsewhere, at http://ocoy.org/podcasts/

Reading for Awakening

Light of the Spirit Press presents books on spiritual wisdom and Original Christianity and Original Yoga. From our "Dharma for Awakening" series (practical commentaries on the world's scriptures) to books on how to meditate and live a successful spiritual life, you will find books that are informative, helpful, and even entertaining.

Light of the Spirit Press is the publishing house of Light of the Spirit Monastery (Atma Jyoti Ashram) in Cedar Crest, New Mexico, USA. Our books feature the writings of the founder and director of the monastery, Abbot George Burke (Swami Nirmalananda Giri) which are also found on the monastery's website, OCOY.org.

We invite you to explore our publications in the following pages.

Find out more about our publications at
lightofthespiritpress.com

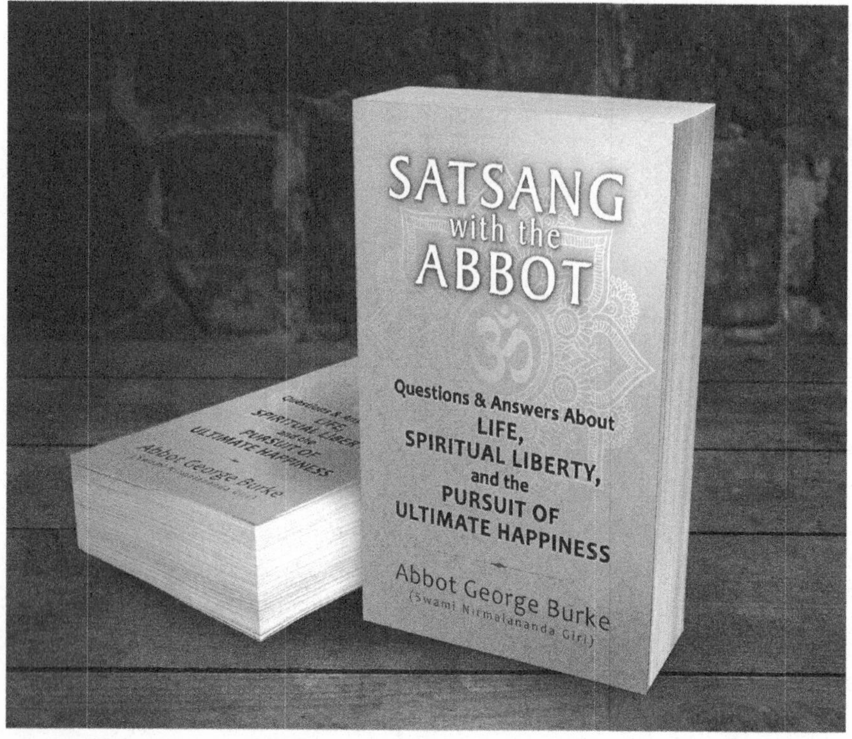

Satsang with the Abbot

Questions & Answers about Life, Spiritual Liberty, and the Pursuit of Ultimate Happiness

> "The scriptures contain a mixture of sand and sugar, as it were. It is extremely difficult to separate the sugar from the sand. Therefore one should learn of the essence of the scriptures from the teacher or from a sadhu. " —Sri Ramakrishna

Abbot George Burke has spent a lifetime helping spiritual aspirants separate the sand from the sugar. Grounded in the perspective of classic Indian thought, directly taught by such luminaries as Swami Sivananda of Rishikesh and Sri Anandamayi Ma, and blessed with the clarity and originality of thought that can only come from years of spiritual practice (sadhana), his answers to his inquirers' questions are unique, fresh, and authoritative.

The questions in this book range from the most sublime to the most practical. "How can I attain samadhi? " "I am married with children. How can I lead a spiritual life? " "What is Self-realization? "

Among these 350+ questions and answers, you will find these topics:

- karma, reincarnation, and spiritual evolution,
- avatars, angels, devas, spirits, ghosts and demons,

- death and the after-life, astral travel, astrology,
- esoteric view of Jesus and Christianity, the "Lost Years," and modern yogis who saw Jesus,
- effective meditation methods, how to deal with the mind, vegetarianism, and practical spirituality,
- stories of Babaji, Yogananda and his disciples, Anandamayi Ma, Sri Ramakrishna and his disciples, and modern saints of India,
- the spiritual principles (dharma) that unite the inner traditions of Hinduism, Buddhism, Christianity and other world religions.

In Abbot George's replies to these questions the reader will discover common sense, helpful information, and a guiding light for their journey through and beyond the forest of cliches, contradictions, and confusion of yoga, Hinduism, Christianity, and metaphysical thought.

What Readers say:

"Abbot George speaks as one who knows his subject well, and answers in an manner that conveys an effortlessness and humor that puts one at ease, while, at the same time, a wisdom and sincerity which demands an attentive ear. "—*Russ Thomas*

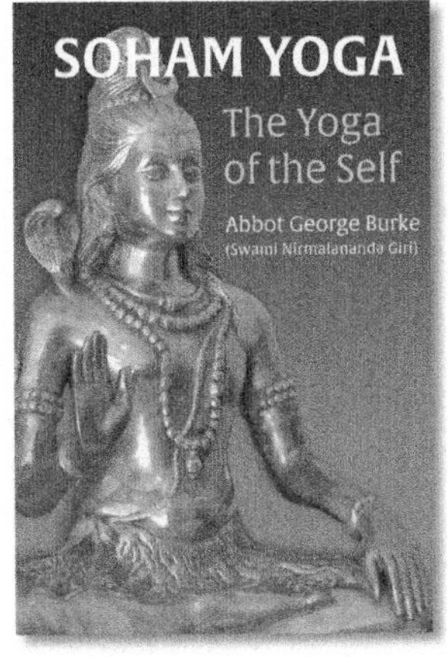

Soham Yoga

The Yoga of the Self

An in-depth guide to the practice of Soham sadhana.

Soham (which is pronounced like "Sohum") means: I Am That. It is the natural vibration of the Self, which occurs spontaneously with each incoming and outgoing breath. By becoming aware of it on the conscious level by mentally repeating it in time with the breath (*So* when inhaling and *Ham* when exhaling), a yogi experiences the identity between his individual Self and the Supreme Self.

The practice is very simple, and the results very profound. Truly wondrous is the fact that Soham Yoga can go on all the time, not just during meditation, if we apply ourselves to it. The whole life can become a continuous stream of liberating sadhana. "By the mantra 'Soham' separate the jivatma from the Paramatma and locate the jivatma in the heart" (Devi Bhagavatam 11.8.15). When we repeat Soham in time with the breath we are invoking our eternal being. This is why we need only listen to our inner mental intonations of Soham in time with the breath which itself is Soham.

What Readers say:

"The more I read this book, study it and practice Soham meditation and japa, the more thrilled I am to find this book. It is a complete spiritual path of Yoga."—*Arnold Van Wie*

Visit sohamyogameditation.com to read online or to download a free PDF.

Also available online in paperback and ebook versions.

The Bhagavad Gita for Awakening

A Practical Commentary for Leading a Successful Spiritual Life

With penetrating insight, Abbot George Burke illumines the Bhagavad Gita's practical value for spiritual seekers. With a unique perspective from a lifetime of study and practice of both Eastern and Western spirituality, Abbot George presents the treasures of the Gita in an easily intelligible fashion.

Drawing from the teachings of Sri Ramakrishna, Jesus, Paramhansa Yogananda, Ramana Maharshi, Swami Vivekananda, Swami Sivananda of Rishikesh, Papa Ramdas, and other spiritual masters and teachers, as well as his own experiences, Abbot Burke illustrates the teachings of the Gita with stories which make the teachings of Krishna in the Gita vibrant and living.

What Readers say:

"This is not a book for only "Hindus" or "Christians." Anyone desiring to better their lives mentally, emotionally, and spiritually would benefit greatly by reading this book."— *Sailaja Kuruvadi*

Dwelling in the Mirror

A Study of Illusions Produced by Delusive Meditation and How to Be Free from Them

"There are those who can have an experience and realize that it really cannot be real, but a vagary of their mind. Some may not understand that on their own, but can be shown by others the truth about it. For them and those that may one day be in danger of meditation-produced delusions I have written this brief study." –Abbot George Burke

In *Dwelling in the Mirror* you will learn:

- different types of meditation and the experiences they produce, and the problems and delusions which can arise from them.
- how to get rid of negative initiation energies and mantras.
- what are authentic, positive meditation practices and their effects and aspects.
- an ancient, universal method of meditation which is both proven and effective.

What Readers say:

"I totally loved this book! After running across many spiritual and self-help books filled with unrealistic promises, this little jewel had the impact of a triple Espresso."—Sandra Carrington-Smith, author of *Housekeeping for the Soul*

The Christ of India

The Story of Original Christianity

"Original Christianity" is the teaching of both Jesus of Nazareth and his Apostle Saint Thomas in India. Although it was new to the Mediterranean world, it was really the classical, traditional teachings of the ancient rishis of India that even today comprise Sanatana Dharma, the Eternal Dharma, that goes far beyond religion into realization.

In The Christ of India Abbot George Burke presents what those ancient teachings are, as well as the growing evidence that Jesus spent much of his "Lost Years" in India and Tibet. This is also the story of how the original teachings of Jesus and Saint Thomas thrived in India for centuries before the coming of the European colonialists.

What Readers say:

"Interpreting the teachings of Jesus from the perspective of Santana Dharma, The Christ of India is a knowledgeable yet engaging collection of authentic details and evident manuscripts about the Essene roots of Jesus and his 'Lost years'. ...delightful to read and a work of substance, vividly written and rich in historical analysis, this is an excellent work written by a masterful teacher and a storyteller." *–Enas Reviews*

The Dhammapada for Awakening

A Commentary on Buddha's Practical Wisdom

The Dhammapada for Awakening brings a refreshing and timely perspective to ancient wisdom and shows seekers of inner peace practical ways to improve their inner lives today.

It explores the Buddha's answers to the urgent questions, such as "How can I find find lasting peace, happiness and fulfillment that seems so elusive?" and "What can I do to avoid many of the miseries big and small that afflict all of us?".

Drawing on the proven wisdom of different ancient traditions, and the contemporary masters of spiritual life, as well as his own studies and first-hand knowledge of the mystical traditions of East and West, Abbot George illumines the practical wisdom of Buddha in the Dhammapada, and more importantly, and make that makes that teaching relevant to present day spiritual seekers.

What Readers say:

"In this compelling book, Abbot George Burke brings his considerable knowledge and background in Christian teachings and the Vedic tradition of India to convey a practical understanding of the teachings of the Buddha. ...This is a book you'll want to take your time to read and keep as reference to reread. Highly recommended for earnest spiritual aspirants" *–Anna Hourihan, author, editor, and publisher at Vedanta Shores Press*

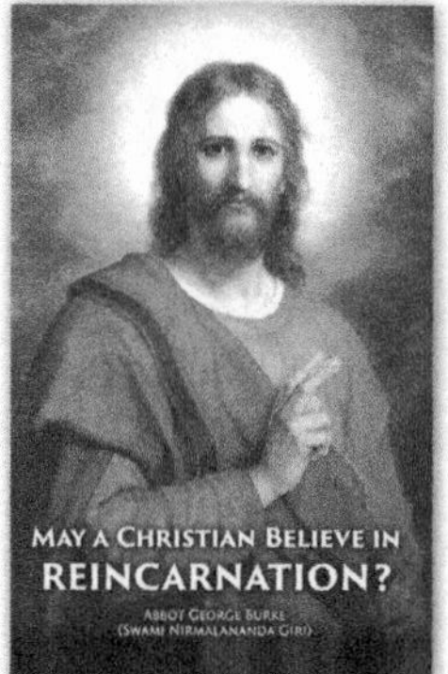

May a Christian Believe in Reincarnation?

Discover the real and surprising history of reincarnation and Christianity.

A growing number of people are open to the subject of past lives, and the belief in rebirth–reincarnation, metempsychosis, or transmigration–is becoming commonplace. It often thought that belief in reincarnation and Christianity are incompatible. But is this really true? May a Christian believe in reincarnation? The answer may surprise you.

Reincarnation-also known as the transmigration of souls-is not just some exotic idea of non-Christian mysticism. Nor is it an exclusively Hindu-Buddhist teaching.

In orthodox Jewish and early Christian writings, as well as the Holy Scriptures, we find reincarnation as a fully developed belief, although today it is commonly ignored. But from the beginning it has been an integral part of Orthodox Judaism, and therefore as Orthodox Jews, Jesus and his Apostles would have believed in rebirth.

What Readers say:

"Those needing evidence that a belief in reincarnation is in accordance with teachings of the Christ need look no further: Plainly laid out and explained in an intelligent manner from one who has spent his life on a Christ-like path of renunciation and prayer/meditation." —*Christopher T. Cook*

A Brief Sanskrit Glossary
A Spiritual Student's Guide to Essential Sanskrit Terms

This Sanskrit glossary contains full translations and explanations of many of the most commonly used spiritual Sanskrit terms, and will help students of the Bhagavad Gita, the Upanishads, the Yoga Sutras of Patanjali, and other Indian scriptures and philosophical works to expand their vocabularies to include the Sanskrit terms contained in them, and gain a fuller understanding in their studies.

What Readers say:

"If you are reading the writings of Swami Sivananda you will find a basketful of untranslated Sanskrit words which often have no explanation, as he assumes his readers have a background in Hindu philosophy. For writings like his, this book is invaluable, as it lists frequently used Sanskrit terms used in writings on yoga and Hindu philosophical thought.

"As the title says, this is a spiritual students' guidebook, listing not only commonly used spiritual terms, but also giving brief information about spiritual teachers and writers, both modern and ancient.

"Abbot George's collection is just long enough to give the meanings of useful terms without overwhelming the reader with an overabundance of extraneous words. This is a book that the spiritual student will use frequently."—*Simeon Davis*

The Gospel of Thomas for Awakening

A Commentary on Jesus' Sayings as Recorded by the Apostle Thomas

"From the very beginning there were two Christianities." So begins this remarkable work. While the rest of the Apostles dispersed to various areas of the Mediterranean world, the apostle Thomas travelled to India, where growing evidence shows that Jesus spent his "Lost Years," and which had been the source of the wisdom which he had brought to the "West."

In *The Gospel of Thomas for Awakening,* Abbot George shines the "Light of the East" on the sometimes enigmatic sayings of Jesus recorded by his apostle Saint Thomas, revealing their unique and rich practical nature for modern day seekers for spiritual life.

Ideal for daily study or group discussion.

What Readers say:

"An extraordinary work of theological commentary, *The Gospel of Thomas for Awakening* is as informed and informative as it is inspired and inspiring".—*James A. Cox, Editor-in-Chief, Midwest Book Review*

The Bhagavad Gita–The Song of God

A new translation of the most important spiritual classic which India has produced.

Often called the "Bible" of Hinduism, the Bhagavad Gita is found in households throughout India and has been translated into every major language of the world. Literally billions of copies have been handwritten and printed.

The clarity of this translation by Abbot George Burke makes for easy reading, while the rich content makes this the ideal "study" Gita. As the original Sanskrit language is so rich, often there are several accurate translations for the same word, which are noted in the text, giving the spiritual student the needed understanding of the fullness of the Gita.

For those unable to make a spiritual journey to India, a greater pilgrimage can be made by anyone anywhere in the world by simply reading The Holy Song of God, the Srimad Bhagavad Gita. It will be a holy pilgrimage of mind and spirit.

Robe of Light

An Esoteric Christian Cosmology

In *Robe of Light* Abbot George Burke explores the whys and wherefores of the mystery of creation. From the emanation of the worlds from the very Being of God, to the evolution of the souls to their ultimate destiny as perfected Sons of God, the ideal progression of creation is described. Since the rebellion of Lucifer and the fall of Adam and Eve from Paradise flawed the normal plan of evolution, a restoration was necessary. How this came about is the prime subject of this insightful study.

Moreover, what this means to aspirants for spiritual perfection is expounded, with a compelling knowledge of the scriptures and of the mystical traditions of East and West.

What Readers say:

"Having previously read several offerings from the pen of Abbot George Burke I was anticipating this work to be well written and an enjoyable read. However, Robe of Light actually exceeded my expectations. Abbot Burke explicates the subject perfectly, making a difficult and complex subject like Christian cosmology accessible to those of us who are not great theologians."—*Russ Thomas*

Foundations of Yoga

Ten Important Principles Every Meditator Should Know

An in-depth examination of the important foundation principles of Patanjali's Yoga, Yama & Niyama.

Yama and Niyama are often called the Ten Commandments of Yoga, but they have nothing to do with the ideas of sin and virtue or good and evil as dictated by some cosmic potentate. Rather they are determined on a thoroughly practical, pragmatic basis: that which strengthens and facilitates our yoga practice should be observed and that which weakens or hinders it should be avoided.

It is not a matter of being good or bad, but of being wise or foolish. Each one of these Five Don'ts (Yama) and Five Do's (Niyama) is a supporting, liberating foundation of Yoga. An introduction to the important foundation principles of Patanjali's Yoga: Yama & Niyama

Available as a free Kindle ebook download at Amazon.com, as well as in paperback.

Spiritual Benefits
of a Vegetarian Diet
Abbot George Burke
(Swami Nirmalananda Giri)

Spiritual Benefits of a Vegetarian Diet

The health benefits of a vegetarian diet are well known, as are the ethical aspects. But the spiritual advantages should be studied by anyone involved in meditation, yoga, or any type of spiritual practice.

Although diet is commonly considered a matter of physical health alone, since the Hermetic principle "as above, so below" is a fundamental truth of the cosmos, diet is a crucial aspect of emotional, intellectual, and spiritual development as well. For diet and consciousness are interrelated, and purity of diet is an effective aid to purity and clarity of consciousness.

The major thing to keep in mind when considering the subject of vegetarianism is its relevancy in relation to our explorations of consciousness. We need only ask: Does it facilitate my spiritual growth–the development and expansion of my consciousness? The answer is Yes.

A second essay, *Christian Vegetarianism,* continues with a consideration of the esoteric side of diet, the vegetarian roots of early Christianity, and an insightful exploration of vegetarianism in the Old and New Testaments.

Available as a free Kindle ebook download at Amazon.com.

Notes

Made in the USA
Las Vegas, NV
22 November 2023